NOAKHALI TO INFINITY

DEEPANKAR NARAYAN ROY

INDIA • SINGAPORE • MALAYSIA

Notion Press

Old No. 38, New No. 6
McNichols Road, Chetpet
Chennai - 600 031

First Published by Notion Press 2018
Copyright © Deepankar Narayan Roy 2018
All Rights Reserved.

ISBN 978-1-64429-365-2

Contents

Bhulua Pargana

At the beginning of 13 centuries, Bhulua, a new kingdom, was founded by Biswambhar Sur, ex-ruler of Mithila, in Samatata Janapada, in the Bengal's eastern zone. He and his descendants reigned over the Bhulua territories independently for several centuries. Later, their descendants ruled the Bhulua as a vassal of Bengal Sultanate, thereafter Mughal Subadhar and at last East India Company. At first, it was a Hindu kingdom and all the subjects were Hindus. Afterwards, most of the indigenous people of the soil were converted to Islam, but the Kings remained Hindu and they ruled the territory from the 13th century AD to the 19th century AD. *Kings of Srirampur part of Bhulua* lived and ruled their kingdom from **Srirampur Rajbari.** The members of the **Rajbari** considered their ancestral homeland as an *El Dorado*, a longed-for land flowing with milk and honey. *They* were compelled to leave their homeland because of the partition of Bengal that triggered off a wave of rioting. The Rajbar's family members experienced serious human rights abuses since 16/08/1946, the Direct Action Day. Villages of Noakhali looked like a Nazi concentration camp, Buchenwald in Germany, since 10 October 1946, the day in which the acts of pro-Pakistan riots started.

After fleeing from their homeland, the older members of Roy families felt that their feet left Noakhali, but not their heart. They did not just escape Noakhali; they had to escape a thousand memories. They adored not only the place but also cherished its flora and fauna, dialect and so on, they loved their native land until their last breath. All the trivial matters in the native land boosted their happiness.

I Shall Return Once More–Jibanananda Das.

> **"Again, I shall return to the Dhansiri's banks,** to this Bengal, Not as a man, perhaps, but as a shalik bird, or a white hawk. As, perhaps, a crow of dawn in this land of autumn's new rice harvest, I'll float upon the breast of fog one day in the shade of a jackfruit tree."

Dhansiri is a river in Bangladesh, Shalik is another name for a Maina bird, and Jibananda Das (1899-1954) is a premier poet of the post-Tagore era in India.

> "Sweet, sweet home!
> There's no place like home
> there's no place like home!
> An exile from home splendour dazzles in vain
> Oh; give me my lowly thatched cottage again.
> The birds singing gaily that came at my call
> and gave me the peace of mind dearer than all
> Home, home, sweet, sweet home
> there's no place like home, there's no place like home."

– John Howard Payne (1791-1852)

Bhulua was the youngest among the districts in the Brahmaputra Delta that rose out of the sea. Several enormous rivers flow through the Brahmaputra Delta, including Padma and Jamuna, which merge with the Meghna and passed across Bhulua before entering the Bay of Bengal. The areas are 3000 years old since it became fit for human habitation. The silt and sediment deposition of Padma, Brahmaputra (Jamuna) and Meghna Rivers formed the deltaic floodplain of Bhulua. It comprised jungles and wetlands for several centuries.

Aboriginal inhabitants (Proto Australoid) of the adjacent areas were the early settlers on this swamp island of the Meghna. In Aryan mythology and ancient records, there has been no reference to Bhulua or Noakhali or its inhabitants. Non-Aryan people inhabited the ancient Bengal. The earliest known religion of Bengal was the non-Vedic form of Hinduism. The Indo-Aryans migrations happened during the post-Gupta period, i.e. in the 6th century. After the arrival of Indo-Aryans, religion was a composite mixture of old Hinduism and a new Vedic religion. Hindu castes system travelled to Samatata probably around the 13th century.

The ancient land of Bengal was divided among various tribes or kingdoms, which were known as Janapadas or human settlements. The ancient Janapadas in Bengal are Harikela, Samatata, Vanga, and Varendra. Vanga is believed to be central Bengal, Harikela, and Samatata were Bengal's eastern zones and Varendra was northern Bengal.

The trans-Meghna territories of the Comilla Noakhali plains at the mouth of the Meghna Brahmaputra River were known as Samatata Janapada. It was by the side of the Harikela Janapada (Chittagong district).

The 7th-century Chinese traveller visited many sacred Buddhist sites and described Samatata as a low coastal delta land and a Buddhist cultural centre. A large Buddhist monastery dating between the 6th to 12th centuries A. D in the Lalmai-Mainamati area was discovered during the second world wartime in the Samatata region. It was a centre of Buddhist civilization before the rebirth of Hinduism and thereafter, it was the place for new beginning of Islam. Conversion to Islam was more common where Buddhism had once been stronger.

The Lalmai-Mainamati- the religious centre from which Buddhism was spread to South East Asia.

Bengal was divided into several independent kingdoms for most of its history. It was unified only a few times. Samatata region was a vassal or feudatory of the Gupta Empire. After the fall of the Gupta Empire, a *local ruler, King Shashanka,* united the Bengal for the *first time.* With the collapse of his Kingdom, Bengal split up into small kingdoms once more. The different Hindu or Muslim rulers or Baro Bhuiyan of Bengal, ruled different Janapada either independently or being a vassal of the Mughal emperor or Bengal Sultanates or the British during the entire period from 13th century onwards.

King Biswambhar Sur and his descendants reigned over Bhulua Pargana from 1203 to 1611 A D. From the late 16th to early 17th centuries, the Subedar of the Mughal Empire ruled Bengal. Then, from 1611 A D to 1717 A. D, Bhulua was ruled by Sur rulers accepting the feudatory of the Mughal Subedar. The gradual decline of the Mughal Empire led to make different quasi-independent Kingdoms, and Bhulua became a vassal of Nawabs of Bengal from 1717 to 1765. The East India Company captured Noakhali in 1765. Royal families then ruled part of Bhulua under the East India Company up to 1833. In 1833, the East India Company auctioned the estate of the Srirampur family to recover their arrear taxes. Thereafter, the descendants of Biswambhar Sur were a subject of new Zamindar, Rani Katyayani, wife of Lala Babu, the Zamindar of Kandi in Murshidabad.

In 1857, the British Crown assumed direct control of India from the East India Company. The East India Company was a British Joint Stock Company. The trading farm took command of an entire sub-continent which had a whole variety of shareholders; Marwari people were the shareholders of the East India Company. Marwari capital based in Bengal in the 18th Century was crucial behind the rise of the East India Company and its later dominion over all of Mughal India, author

William Dalrymple argued, in a talk in New Delhi, speaking during a book tour to promote his new book 'The Anarchy'. He said, "This comes as a surprise to most Indians, but Marwari businessmen and their capital aided the East India Company."

200 hundred years ago, we knew the greater Noakhali as Bhulua Pargana. It comprised the present Bhola and Lakshmipur districts, the mainland of the Noakhali district, and a part of the present Feni district.

Floodwaters of the Dakaita River affected the Agricultural activities of Bhulua. To salvage the situation, digging of a canal was begun in the year 1660 A. D from the Dakaita through Ramganj, Sonaimuri, and Chowmuhani to divert the water flow to the junction of Meghna River and Feni. The labour problems and a cholera epidemic slowed the construction. After excavating this long canal, we knew Bhulua as "Noakhali" from the term Noa (New) and Khal (Canal). So, *they renamed Bhulua Pargana as Noakhali in 1868 A. D. In 1984 A. D, greater Noakhali was divided into three districts, Noakhali, Feni, and Lakshmipur.*

Noakhali Just Before Independence in 1947

Noakhali is one of the esturian districts, where communication for a long part of the year is using the waterways. It has a long coastline with the Meghna estuary and is often subject to tidal waves and cyclones originated in the Bay of Bengal. The district comprises a tract of mainland together with many islands in the mouth of the Meghna, the largest of which are Sandip and Hatia.

Eighty percent of the population of Noakhali was Muslims; the remaining population was mostly lower caste Hindus and Dalit in an agrarian society. Upper caste Hindus and minuscule of Muslim families owned most land properties and controlled the agrarian economy. The Noakhali was a renowned centre of orthodox Islam. It was the district that sent most of the Muslim priest and preacher to the rest of the Bengal. There were extreme class and religious divisions and rigid social mobility. Before the independence, the situation in Noakhali became very tense because of the religious war cry given by the Muslim League for the Tehrik-e-Pakistan or the Pakistan movement. The fundamentalist forces became active with anti-Hindu propaganda under the leadership of prominent Muslim League leaders.

On 10th Oct 1946, on the night of Kojagari Lakshmi Puja, the Goddess of prosperity, when most of the lands in Noakhali District were still underwater, and most of the Hindus were busy in their household with Lakshmi Puja's ritual, fanatic communal forces started a deliberate genocide upon the minority Hindu community.

A series of massacres, rapes, abduction, forced conversion to Islam, looting, and arson on Hindus and their properties continued for a week to avenge the Great Calcutta killings on the Direct Action Day.

In 1946, Muhammad Ali Jinnah declared 16 August as Direct Action Day to put pressure on the British government to divide the country based on religion.

The Direct Action Day sparked off riots between Hindus and Muslims in Calcutta. H. S. Suhrawardy, the ruthless Muslim League Chief Minister of Bengal, was accused of allowing riots to support his party's demand for partition and made provoking speeches against his Hindu populace.

The estimated 5000 Hindus were killed in a week in the Noakhali Genocide. Minority Hindus were hounded out of their houses by a group of Muslim fanatics just like what happened to Jews in Hitler's Germany. The organized Muslim mob perpetrated loot, arson, and killing allying with political and religious organizations. The Muslim Superintendent of police played a part in encouraging the rowdies by his complete inactivity. Some even said that his co-operation was not always passive but active at a time. There were religious conversion camps in affected areas instead of concentration camps in Germany. Thousands of Hindu men and women were forcibly converted to Islam and a hundred Hindu women were raped. The outside world was, however, kept in the dark about the events for a week. The government blacked out all news of the genocide. News of carnage in Noakhali became known to people on 17 October 1946, after seven days of the massacres through press reports.

It would be wrong to say that the Muslim peasants living in the villages of Noakhali were ferocious or criminal by nature. They were as simple and as kind as their brothers in West Bengal. People with a vested interest used them to exploit their ignorance and fanatic devotion to religion for ulterior motives. The mastermind behind the Noakhali riots was Muslim League leader, Gholam Sarwar Husseini, a close associate of Chief Minister of Bengal, Suhrawardy. There are many letters which exist in the National Archives in India and UK, written by Suhrawardy to Husseini urging the letter to start a direct action against Hindus in Noakhali.

The Great Migration of Bengali Hindus

Gandhiji left Sodepur Khadi Ashram **on the 6th of November 1946** for riot devastated Noakhali with his followers to cool the communal situation. The Govt of Bengal had provided a special train fitted with a microphone for Gandhi and his party. Gandhi reached Goalundo Ghat at half-past three on the 6th of November 1946 and addressed a gathering from the deck of the steamer. The Government had kept ready a special streamer for carrying the party 80 miles down the river to Chandpur. Gandhiji and his followers reached Chandpur in the evening and left Chandpur by train at about 10 on the following morning for Chowmuhani. He stayed in Chowmuhani in Noakhali from the 7th to the 9th of November 1946 and then moved on to a village named Duttapara where 6000 Hindu refugees had taken shelter. Wherever he went, he visited the adjacent villages to see the wanton destruction of life and properties to which the areas were subjected. He reached Kazirkhil on 14th Nov 1946 in the late evening and stayed there for seven nights. Mahatma Gandhi set off for Srirampur village and left the house of Kashi Pandit in Kazirkhil at 11.37 a.m. on 20 November 1946 and took a boat to go to Srirampur by the river which was about four miles away. It took over two-and-a-half hours to cover the distance of four miles because of heavy water hyacinth. Gandhiji reached the landing places at Srirampur at 2 p.m. from where the **Srirampur Rajbari** where he would be camped was only a furlong away. Thus, Gandhiji's life began in the village of Srirampur, where he was alone, and he had sent away all his followers. Gandhiji wanted to face Noakhali individually. He camped at Roy family's ancestral home from 20th of Nov 1946 to 1st of January 1947, i.e. for 43 nights. **On January 1, 1947**, the last day of Gandhi's six weeks stay in *Srirampur Rajbari*, he began his usual evening prayer mass by saying that his stay in that village had been enriched by the abundance of love shown to him by the members of the family in whose midst he had been living. Then a verse of Gita was recited. Before the departure from Srirampur Rajbari the next morning, he offered Ramayana epic as a memento to elderly members of the house and the book bore the inscription written by Gandhi himself.

This was his longest stay at any place in Bengal. During that period, Hindu and Muslim leaders came to the house to meet with him. Gandhi Maharaj also visited vandalized houses and victimized families to cool down their raw nerves in the affected areas. He wrote to Premier Suhrawardy, the last Chief Minister of Bengal during the British Raj (3 December 1946), "The (Peace) Committees do not appear to be functioning properly, the exodus continues."

On 19th December, after he had been a month in Srirampur, Manuben, the grandniece of Gandhi arrived in Srirampur Rajbari. She was always at Gandhi's side as his 'walking stick'. Manuben in her diary noted on 28th December 1946, 9 days after joining the then 77-year-old Gandhi in Srirampur Rajbari that "Bapu is a mother to me. He is initiating me to a higher human plane through the Brahmacharya experiments, part of his Maha Yagna of character-building. Any loose talk about the experiment is most condemnable." After joining Srirampur, she had taken charge to look after the Gandhiji.

On 27 Dec 1946, Pandit Nehru, J.P. Kripalani, Sucheta Kripalani, S. Deo, and Mridula Sarabhai arrived half-past eleven at night in Srirampur Rajbari to meet Mahatma to know his views about the constituent assembly.

Pandit Nehru and Acharya Kripalani, the two leaders, urged Gandhiji to return to Delhi, but Gandhiji did not agree. On the morning of 30 December 1946, Congress leaders left Srirampur Rajbari for Delhi. They went to Madhupur on foot, from where the jeep carried them to Feni, the airport.

Gandhi's stay in Noakhali displeased Muslim leadership. On 12 February 1947, while addressing a rally in Comilla, A. K. Fazlul Huq first elected Prime Minister of Bengal and a distinguished lawyer who served as General Secretary of the Indian National Congress and was a working committee member of the All India Muslim League, stated in a public meeting that Gandhi's presence in Noakhali harmed communal harmony. His presence had caused the bitter relationship between Hindus and Muslims. The resentment against Gandhi's stay in Noakhali escalated day by day. Towards the end of February 1947, the situation worsened. His path was deliberately dirtied every day, and the Muslims boycotted his meetings. Gandhi took a goat from India. He kept that she-goat with him in Noakhali as he used to consume goat's milk. Local Muslims stole that goat and ate it. ***Gandhi discontinued his mission halfway and started for Bihar on 2 March 1947 at the call of the Muslim League leaders.*** He went to Bihar to ensure that the minority Muslims there were not being treated like the minority Hindus in Noakhali. During his stay in Noakhali, he covered 116 miles and visited 47 villages. Observing vast massacres, he said: "My heart bleeds; my brain is strained to think that the East Bengal Hindus who were in the vanguard in the struggle for freedom will be deprived of their ancestral home and hearth."

The rioting mob killed Lalmohan Sen, a revolutionary who had taken part in the Chittagong Armoury Raid on 18 April 1930 and imprisoned for 16 years by the British.

On April 7, more than a month after his leaving, Gandhi received telegrams from Congress party workers in Noakhali, describing attempts to burn Hindus alive. He stated that the situation in Noakhali demanded that the Hindus should either leave or perish.

> ## QUIT NOAKHALI OR DIE, GANDHI WARNS HINDUS
>
> NEW DELHI, India, April 7 (AP) —Mohandas K. Gandhi, who has been attempting to insure communal peace in the Bengal and Bihar areas, said today religious strife in the troubled Noakhali section of Bengal seemed to call for Hindus to leave or perish "in the flames of fanaticism."

He was successful in establishing peace and communal harmony in Calcutta, but not in Noakhali and East Bengal. Nirmal Kumar Bose recorded in his book *"My days with Gandhi"* [Gandhi mutters to himself one day in Srirampur] "What shall I do? What shall I do?" [To Nirmal Kumar Bose] "I don't want to die a failure. But I may be a failure."

Noakhali was in horrible, horrific and terrible conditions as over 40 Hindus dominated villages had been burnt and communal disturbances were on the rise. Around 50,000 to 75,000 survivors were sheltered in temporary relief camps in Comilla, Chandpur, Agartala, and other places. Apart from that, around 50,000 Hindus that remained marooned in the affected areas were under the strict surveillance of the Muslim fanatic.

Leela Roy recovered about 1307, raped and abducted Hindu girls. Nobody knew about the women who went missing during the organized fury of the Muslim mob. Ashoka Gupta led volunteers for relief works. But atrocities against Hindus were increasing day after day. They forced the Hindus to pay a subscription to the Muslim League as jizya tax as protection money.

"The world will not be destroyed by those who do evil, but by those who watch them doing nothing."

– Albert Einstein

Srirampur Rajbari

A few months after Gandhi's departure, violence erupted again. Society sees women as the repositories of family or community's honour. So violation of the honour of the women signifies an attack upon the honour of the entire community. When Noakhali's situation went from bad to worse, when life and honour of women were at stake, then family members of Rajbari emigrated from Srirampur, became a part of the disordered Hindu refugee crowd and walked towards West Bengal with painful memories of atrocities. The East Bengal's Hindus became refugees during the Swaraj (self-rule) by a tryst with destiny, while the world was sleeping; the refugees were wide awake and crossed the border (Radcliffe line) to save life, religion and the honour of their daughters, wives, and sisters. They had left their entire lives behind, only with just the clothes on their backs. By the religion-based partition of Bengal, East Bengal Hindus became refugees and they lost their ancestral land, honour, identity, liberty, the right to life, the right to live with dignity, the right to property and every fundamental human right. Freedom, another misunderstood term, means a condition in which it does not infringe on these rights.

In Punjab, partition was accompanied by massive inter-communal violence and atrocities against fleeing refugees on both sides. Indian government expected the population to transfer and took proactive measures. Land plots that were evacuated by Muslims were allotted to incoming Hindu and Sikh refugees.

The government allocated substantial resources for the rehabilitation of refugees in Punjab. In contrast, there was no such planning in the eastern part of the country. Neither Central nor the West Bengal State Government expected any large-scale population exchange, and no coordinated policy was in place to rehabilitate millions of homeless people. The newly independent country had a little resource, and the Central government exhausted it in resettling 7 million refugees in Punjab. Instead of providing rehabilitation, the Indian government tried to stop and even reverse the refugee influx from East Bengal. India and Pakistan signed the Nehru-Liaquat pact on 8th April 1950 to stop any further population exchange between West and East Bengal. Both countries agreed to take the refugees back and return to their property, which they evacuated in their respective countries. But both countries failed to uphold it. Even after it became clear that the refugees were not to be sent back, the governments did not provide any significant help. The government policy of East Bengal refugee rehabilitation was mostly composed of sending them to an empty area, mostly outside of West Bengal. One of the most controversial of such schemes was the Government's decision to settle the refugees by force in Dandakaranya, a barren plot of land in the Baster division in the Chhattisgarh state. Circumstances compelled refugees to stay in various refugee camps in remote, unfamiliar parts of India and West Bengal. Because of religious persecution in East Pakistan and Bangladesh, Hindus continue to flee to India. Most of them settle in the state of West Bengal.

Many refugees without government help settled in almost all the districts of West Bengal and the suburb of Calcutta. Refugees squatted in all vacant areas. Some of these places in the urban town were uninhabitable, but they preferred to settle in urban areas for job opportunities. A significant number also moved to the Barak Valley of Assam and the princely state of Tripura. Some found jobs in factories. Many took small businesses and hawking. Many refugee colonies and camps sprang up in Nadia, 24 Parganas, Hooghly, Cooch Behar, Jalpaiguri, West Dinajpur, Burdwan, and Calcutta and its suburb in West Bengal.

Many years after independence, many East Bengal refugees stay as refugees in many places in India under very deplorable and inhumane conditions. The thousands of East Bengal Hindu refugees were forcibly evicted from the Marichghapi island in the Sunderbans, West Bengal, and the subsequent death of a few by police firing on January 31, 1979, they had migrated from Dandakaranya refugee camps in despair. The survivors were then sent back to Dandakaranya. In East Bengal, the Hindu population before 1946 was 39%, which is now 8.96% of the population of Bangladesh. The recent killing of the secular blogger in Bangladesh was in the news. They were the voice against fundamentalism, extremism, and were even a voice for minority rights.

Gandhiji took an insignificant part in the final negotiations, but his opposition to partition was an open secret. He declared, "Whilst the British power is still functioning in India, its function is not to change the map of India. All it has to do is to withdraw and leave India, carrying out the withdrawal, if possible, in orderly manners, maybe even in chaos by the promised date."

By 1946; Gandhi was a solo force in undivided Indian politics. Mountbatten's task was facilitated because, by March 1947, most Congress leaders had made peace with the partition of India.

For Bengal and Bengalis, 1911 and 1947 were very unfortunate years. In 1911, the British transferred the capital of India from Calcutta to Delhi, and in 1947, a good number of Bengalis were ousted from their native land when we stepped out from British India to independent India. Ashoka Gupta wrote, "I still do not know whether anything as terrible as the partition of India has even taken place in this world." All our efforts during the Noakhali riot came to nought. It broke our hearts. We have lived through a lot of history but never seen such a situation.

It is a pleasant piece of news that a Partition Museum was opened in the Amritsar Town Hall, set up by the Arts and Cultural Heritage Trust (TAACHT).

All religions spoke for fellowship, love, peace, and compassion. If religion becomes the cause of hostility and suffering of the people, then it is not needed. If religion aggravates human relations and harmony, then it becomes unnecessary. No religion teaches anybody to hate anyone and to fight in the name of religion

Lennon called for peace and wrote 'imagine' in 1971. The song imagines an imaginary world wherein there will be no countries, no religion, no poverty, no possessions; a world where all the people share the entire world.

JOHN LENNON

"Imagine"

Imagine there's no heaven
It's easy if you try
No hell below us
Above us only sky
Imagine all the people living for today

Imagine there's no countries
It isn't hard to do
Nothing to kill or die for
And no religion too
Imagine all the people living life in peace,

You

You may say I'm a dreamer
But I'm not the only one
I hope someday you'll join us
And the world will be as one

Imagine no possessions
I wonder if you can

No need for greed or hunger
A brotherhood of man
Imagine all the people Sharing all the world, you

You may say I'm a dreamer
But I'm not the only one
I hope someday you'll join us
And the world will be as one.

The well-known science fiction writer Ron Hubbard once said, "If you want to make big money, start a religion." Six years later, Hubbard started a religion of his own: the Church of Scientology. It had about 2, 00,000 followers worldwide, including celebrities like Tom Cruise and John Travolta. Hubbard became wealthy and powerful.

Pseudo saints, Asaram Bapu, and Dr Ram Rahim Insan's episode in India have been another example of Hubbard's belief. They had over two core followers worldwide. Various gods-men have multi-core empires in India and outside. God, if exists, he/she does not follow any religion.

Beginning of the Sur (Roy) Dynasty in Bhulua

At the beginning of the 13th century, Muhammad Bakhtiyar Khilji, a Turkic tribe of Afghanistan, conquered part of eastern India (1203–1206) and became the first Muslim ruler of Bengal. The first establishment of Muslim rule in Eastern India was because of his effort. He was also responsible for the destruction of Nalanda University, and other Buddhist establishments in Eastern India. During his rule, the greatest number of local people converted to Islam. His invasion ushered an era of Muslim rules lasting over five centuries. The Prithviraj Chauhan defeat led to Muslim rule in North India under the Delhi Sultanate (1206-1526).

According to local history, after being overthrown by Bakhtiyar Khilji, Raja Biswambhar Sur, the ninth son of Adi Sur, the king of Mithila, fled from his country and established a new kingdom in the Samatata region in the year 1203 A. D. The new kingdom was known as Bhulua, the ancient name of greater Noakhali.

There was an interesting story behind the name of Bhulua. It was said that King Biswambhar Sur, after being overthrown by Khilji, went on a pilgrimage to Sitakunda Chandranath Temple (one of the oldest Shiva temples in the subcontinent) at Chittagong by sea. They conducted the tour with 149 boats, 200 soldiers, and so many relatives, friends, and families along with priests and royal employees.

In the third week of January 1203 A. D, during his return journey from the holy place, sailors lost their direction while sailing on the sea and moved into an unknown place in the afternoon. Boats stopped in the estuarine sediments where the widest part of the Meghna River met the Bay of Bengal. Ferry-men used all their navigation skills, but they did not get out of the sandbar. They lost all hope and dropped the anchor and stopped. There was no sign of human habitation in that area. Boats got stuck in the estuary sand for over four days. The unknown area was foggy and freezing. All that was visible was marshy land and sandy dunes. The men and women flock of Biswambhar Sur were resting in the boats for the four nights and they knew they were in danger. The king was also alarmed for the safety of his family, royal workers, and troops. On the fifth day, evening, on 1ˢᵗ Magha, 610 Banggabda, Saturday, (16ᵗʰ January 1203 A. D), the ladies blew the conch shell (Shankha) with ululation and worshipped God for their protection and safety. The elderly women and children cried inside the boats in fear.

Biswambhar Sur sat on his boat alone and prayed to God. He fell asleep while praying. The King dreamed a dream in which Goddess Maa Barahi appeared to him and said, "My idol is in the sand where your boats are immobilized. Free me from the sand and do my *Puja* (worship me). You will get the sovereignty of this place. Your descendants up to the 8ᵗʰ generation would rule the areas uninterrupted. From the 9ᵗʰ generation, your progeny would face outside interference and rule part of your kingdom, and after the 12ᵗʰ generation, they would be no more Rulers." God spoke through a dream to some people.

Biswambhar Sur, his royal employees, and friends searched the areas and unearthed the idol of Goddess Maa Barahi from the sand. The royal priest told King, according to Tantra, Maa Barahi should be worshipped after sunset but before sunrise.

On that chilly winter night, they planned to worship the Goddess. On the shore, the royal priest made a sacrificial offering to Goddess with other religious rites and worshipped the Maa Barahi. Royal ladies and male members actively took part in religious rituals and offered salutation to the Goddess (Anjali) with devotion. Before worshipping the Goddess, royal ladies and males encircled the Maa Barahi 7 times.

When the *Puja* was finished, the sun appeared in the East, then everybody discovered that they placed the sacrificing animal face towards the west instead of east. Then everybody exclaimed in disgust, 'Bhul-Hua'. A mistake happened. From then onwards, the new territory was called Bhulua from Bhul-Hua. Till now, residents of the areas place the face of the sacrificing animal to the west as custom as done by the first King during the Puja of his family deity. The descendants of Biswambhar Sur, then onwards worshipped Maa Barahi as Kuladevi.

Mary Harrsch - originally posted to Flickr, Maa Barahi Devi in the form of a boar 1000-1100 Ce India, Eastern Bihar state Chlorite, housed in the Asian Art Museum of San Francisco.

Agnivanshi Ancestry

Many of the ruling clan groups emerged from Rajputs clan and they had firmly established principalities mainly in north-west, east, and northeast part of India. Adi Sur was said to have been of Rajput extraction, an Agnivanshi lineage, claiming to be a descent from Agni (Fire), the Vedic God of fire. Four Rajput clans are considered Agnivanshi. They are Chauhans, Parihars, Solankis, and Parmars. A possibility exists that Sur is one of the 24 branches of the Chauhan tribe. However, this has not been proven. Sur (Soor) is most likely derived from the word "shoor," which means "brave." Some Surs nowadays state that Sur is a shortened version of "Surya," meaning the Sun. However, it was observed that Biswambhar or his descendants married the Kayastha caste and at present the Sur is Kayastha. Maybe Rajput clans were absent in the Samatata region, so it compelled them to marry the Bengali Kayastha. It was stated that Kalyanpur was the capital of Raja Biswambhar Sur, but the author of the "Rajmala" (a chronicle book about the Kings of Tripura) suggests Amishapara was a more likely place for capital because this village contained a Temple of Maa Barahi, kuldevi of the Sur dynasty. In 1946, during the Noakhali riot, Muslim fundamentalists raided the temple, plundered its wealth, and tried to break the Maa Barahi idol.

The head priest of the temple carried the original statue of the Goddess Barahi in India, stuffed it in between clothes and other items.

But the present whereabouts of Maa Barahi in West Bengal was unknown. A temple of Maa Barahi was still present at Amishapara in the Noakhali district, but the idol of God is not the original one.

Whatever it might be, a new kingdom was born in the year 1203 AD. High tides swamped the coast. The area was mostly swamp, uninhabited, and unremarkable until 1203 before the Biswambhar Sur developed the areas. The king invited upper-caste families from different places in his new Kingdom. *Jugies* (weavers) and other working classes came in large numbers to an unknown place for a living. Once an uninhabited swamp region became a thriving human habitation, they founded villages and farmed the land. The Kalyanpur village was developed as the capital of the new Bhulua Kingdom. The royal palaces of Kalyanpur and the surrounding areas were eroded long ago by the mighty Meghna in 1873–74. Vagaries of climate changed the landscape of Noakhali repeatedly. Noakhali's vast area vanished into Meghna in 1873–74; 1918, 1922; 1930; 1932; 1946 and 1948–50. Sudharam, the old headquarters of Noakhali, vanished into the mighty river in 1951. After that, the headquarters of Noakhali was shifted to Maijdee. The river changed its main course several times.

Islam was unknown in Bengal at the beginning of the Sur dynasty. The caste system shaped nearly every facet of Hindu life and it was rigidly enforced. The practise of untouchability on persons because of birth into a lower-caste or Dalit remained a part of Hindu social life. The caste discriminations were very prevalent in Bhulua. Lower castes, Dalits, and Muslims were considered untouchable by the upper caste people, and they were excluded from social gatherings. They could not enter temples or fetch water from local wells. If lower castes and the Dalits cast their shadow upon the so-called higher castes, it was considered a crime.

They could not wear shoes and cover their upper bodies in the presence of upper caste people. On account of caste and class oppression, some lower caste people converted to Islam by the influences of the missionary activities of Muslim Sufis, facilitated by Bakhtiyar Khilji's conquests and Muslim rules spread across the subcontinent over 500 years till the East Indian Company took their place. The phase of the religious conversion of low-caste Hindus into Muslims happened from 1250 to 1757AD.

There is no nation in the world as racial as India. The racial virus attacked our social system as and when Aryans migrated into the sub continent. The Forward castes enjoyed hegemony over the subaltern people. Some low castes revolted against the oppressive caste system prevailing in Hindu society, and various new non-Vedic religious sects were formed in Bengal. These religious groups did not believe in any caste system or Vedic scriptures viz., Baul, Kartabhaga, Sahajiya, Kalachandi Sampradaya, etc. They did not subscribe to Vedic scarifies, Vedic deities, and their rites and rituals.

In the history of religions, it is rare to find a tradition, the Bauls of Bengal practices, in which women are ritual equal, in which nonprocreative activities is more valuable than the reproductive activities, in which menstruation is both positive, and spiritual, and in which the women's body is sacred and the dwelling place of a deity which is neither male nor female but include aspects of both.

Buddhists also do not believe in the caste system and do not teach about God.

The caste system is the most rigorous, most diabolical system of social stratification ever invented by humans and we, the Hindus developed it, the next was putting this evil system into practice since the time immemorial. In Bengal, approximately 65% of lower castes converted to the Islam during the pre-company period because of caste and class oppression.

The Rise of the Sur Dynasty

Biswambhar Sur's family and his previous life are unclear, but it was recorded in history that he was the founder of the Bhulua kingdom in Samatata Janapada.

Founder King Raja Biswambhar Sur ruled the new Bhulua kingdom from the Kalyanpur, his newly built capital. During his rule, there was no foreign invasion and the King did not also invade its neighbours. *He ruled Bhulua from 1203 to 1250 A.D. The main economic activities were agriculture, weaving, and fishery. Inland trading was conducted primarily through barter.* After the Muslim occupation of western and northern Bengal, many Brahmans and Kayasthas of these localities migrated to Bhulua Pargana accepting the King's invitation which, however, remained under the independent Hindu Kings for four hundred years. The King donated revenue-free land to these invitee Brahmins and other higher caste Hindus for their livelihood.

After the founder King's demise, his elder son, **Raja Ganapati Roy** ascended to the throne of Bhulua in the year *1250 A. D and ruled* until his death in 1300A D. He was a skilful administrator and led a major rebuilding program after his father's reign. During his tenure, no major incidents happened in Bhulua, and the ruler ruled the country peacefully, but the conversion of so-called low caste Hindus and Dalits to Muslim religion got started by the Muslim Sufi mystics of Arabia. Bengal was then a wealthy province and generated 24.4% of the world's GDP in 1700 A D.

Trade relations existed between the Indian Subcontinent and Arabia since ancient times, and Muslim Sufis arrived in the eastern part of India by ships through the Chittagong port with the Arab merchants and traders to propagate the Islam religion. They went to the remotest corners of rural Bhulua to promote their religion. They succeeded to convert low caste Hindus to Muslims. The unorthodox approach of Sufi mystics made it easier and attractive for low caste Hindus to accept the faith against the prevailing tyrannical Hindu Caste System. Mazar or Dargah in different places in the remotest area in Eastern India, particularly in undivided Bengal, were erected over the grave of Sufi religious figures. The religious conversion was collective rather than the individual, although individual Hindus who became out-caste or who were ostracised for any reason from the caste system often became Muslims. Nobel Laureates Naipaul commented on the conversion of Hindus to Muslims: "It has had a calamitous effect on converted peoples. To be converted, you have to destroy your past, destroy your history. You have to stamp on it, you have to say 'my ancestral culture does not exist, it doesn't matter'."

But, in the 15th century onward, viewing people according to their religion, Hindu Vs Muslim, was something that did not exist. In fact, it did not exist until the 19th century, until the British came to India and developed the system of diving India into Hindu period and Muslim period. In the past, we had a complex identity, so people were linked through the clan, through the community, through trade, through language or locality. People's identify were made in so many ways and their religious identities had no importance at all. They lived together in peace and perfect amity. So, the simplistic way of reducing the people to their religious identity was a British creation. It was the British that constructed Hindu and Muslim identities through the first Census of British India in 1871-1872. The subsequent strife between these groups was a function of this policy.

Raja Ganapati, on his death, was succeeded by his only son, **Raja Shurananda Khan, in 1300** A D. *He ruled Bhulua kingdom up to 1345 A.D.* During his rule, Fakhruddin Mubarak Shah (1338-1349) of Sonargaon, an independent Muslim Sultanate, raided the kingdom and took away a colossal amount of booty from Bhulua.

Raja Shurananda had two sons, elder Sriram Khan and younger Bidyananda Khan. **Sriram Khan** became the 4th king of the Sur dynasty after the death of Raja Shurananda. Raja Sriram Khan built a separate Royal Palace at Srirampur and it was known as Srirampur Rajbari and the village was named after the King. The royal palace was also served as a fort, so it was also called Srirampur Killabari or Srirampur Fort. Srirampur Rajbari is one among a handful of the former royal house in Bengal. Mahatma Gandhi camped in this house for 43 days during the Pro Pakistan Noakhali riots. It is at present at a Lakshmipur district after bifurcation of the old Noakhali district. *Sriram Khan ruled the Bhulua from 1345 to 1410 A.D.*

Raja Kabi Chandra Khan, the only son of Raja Sriram Khan, had ascended the throne after the demise of Raja Sriram Khan in the year **1410 A.D.** He was a renowned poet in his day.

Some Sur king's titles were Khan. It surprises us to find out that Kayastha Rajas used Muslim surname Khan, and it was used by the 3rd, 4th, and 5th Rajas of the Sur dynasty. During the time, the ruling Hindu kings were awarded the Khan title by Bengal Sultanates as a formal title of respect and honour and the recipient entitled to use the title to his name.

After the demise of Raja Kabichandra Khan, their descendants did not use the Khan title as a surname. They used Roy or Manikya as a surname. It was not true that the descendant of Raja Biswambhar Sur acknowledged the suzerainty of Rajas of Tipperah.

Raja Kabi Chandra ruled the Bhulua Kingdom from 1410 to 1470 A.D. He had two sons. After the death of King, two sons divided the kingdom between themselves. The elder son, Raja **Krishna Chandra Roy,** remained at Srirampur Rajbari or Killabari with 13000 Hajari Jagirdari. The younger son, **Raja Rajballav Roy,** made his Capital at Kalyanpur which was the initial capital of the first King of Bhulua with 13000 Hajari Jagirdari along with 1000 Hajari Jagirdari he gained from his mother. The Bhulua kingdom was now bifurcated into two branches and each branch was ruled individually from Kalyanpur and Srirampur. The family members of both sides kept their relationship alive and attended each other's social occasion.

We know little about the Queens of the Sur dynasty as Hindu women spent most of their time in home confinement. The ladies did not come into public life, and their influence was confined to the family circle. After the Muslim conquests in the Indian Subcontinent, ladies **became *purdahnashins*** (observe the practice of seclusion) and used a *Doli* and sat behind the curtain for movement outside the house. Queens travelled in quite a spacious palanquin with the facility to sleep if travelling was a long journey with the availability of eatables and other necessities with the family members under protecting the royal army.

Every society has dozens of mutually understood preferred way of doing social things such as marriage, the worships of God and last rites of the Individual. The women of the royal families and their descendants practised Maithili social customs, rites, and rituals in their marriages, worships, and last rites ceremonies till today. The old descendants still observed the Maithili traditions in their pristine purity.

The Kalyanpur Branch of the Bhulua's Roy (Manikya) Families

Raja Rajballv Roy, the younger son of Raja Kabichandra Khan, who established his capital at Kalyanpur after bifurcation of Bhulua, was a weak ruler, and he faced attack from Arakan King and Maghs. He took the help of other Kings to free his country from the aggressors. At the end of the war, he gifted Jogadia taluk to Bura Kha, his Hindu general and Dadra pargana to his Muslim general, as a token of gratitude.

The Noakhali Gazette reports did not support the above facts. **He ruled the Bhulua from 1471to 1540 A.D.**

Raja Rajballv had two sons, the Elder Uday Manikya and the younger Gandharva Manikya. The elder son had no child. **Famous Raja Lakshman Manikya** was the son of the younger brother Raja Gandharva Manikya. The most successful king amongst the King's of Bhulua was Raja Lakshman Manikya, who was the 8th descendants of the founder King of Bhulua. **He was also one of the Baro Bhuyan** (twelve territorial landholders) of Bengal who maintained the independent Kingdom against the Mughal Empire and ruled from the middle of the **16th century to**

the early 17th century (1564-1609). He was a contemporary of Mughal emperor Akbar (1556-1605), Isa Khan of Bikrampur and Kandarpa Narayan Bose of Barisal, then known as Chandradwip–Bakla.

King Lakshman Manikya encountered with persistent natural calamities of Meghna & Dakatia Rivers and had rivals like the pirates of the Arkan, the Tripura Rajas, Chandradwip Kings, Portuguese Maghs, and above all the Muslim Nawabs. He brought upper castes Hindus from different places and settled them in his kingdom. He had the noble and cultured courtiers in his court and was himself the author of two Sanskrit dramas. These are, Vikhyata Vijay, based on the battle of Karna and Arjuna as related to the Mahabharata and Kuvalayasva- Charita, based on the story of Madalasa and Kuvalayasva as related in the Mahabharata. His son, Amar Manikya, composed of Vaikuntha-Vijaya and a court poet, Kavitarkik, composed Autuka-Ratnakara. Lakshman Manikya was the last independent king of this dynasty.

The Magh Pirates always disturbed the local Hindu population, and if they walked through anyone's residence or touched anyone, that person with his family was declared "fallen" by the Hindu society. Because of the fear of the Maghs of Arakan, the Hindus always lived in safe quarters, and it was because of their disturbances that the population of lower Bengal, including the deltoid region and the Sundarban had declined.

During the 16th century, part of the land between Chandradwip and Bhulua got eroded by the turbulence of the mighty Meghna River. Eroded areas caused a border dispute between Bhulua and Chandradwip, as the area was strategically important waterways for both the kingdoms for seaborne trade and naval warfare. King Lakshman Manikya was famous for his bravery, knowledge and was a great military man. He defeated King of Chandradwip two times and hoisted the victory flag of Bhulua in Chandradwip.

His rivalry with Kandarpa Narayan Bose of Chandradwip and his son Ramchandra Bose is still famous in folklore. The rivalry grew because of the border disputes and for a Tantric Brahman named Digvijay Bhattacharya, who was the Kulaguru of Chandradwip Basu dynasty. Digvijay Bhattacharya was from Srihatta. They later settled in the Khapura village within the borders of Chandradwip. King Lakshman Manikya was also his disciple and respected Tantric Digvijay Bhattacharya, so the Manikya wanted him to settle in Bhulua. The result was a bitter rivalry between the two Kingdoms. Then, very young Ramchandra Bose was a king after the demise of his father. One night, the Bhulua King surrounded the Khapura village with 5000 men that were within Ramchandra's territory and carried off Digvijay's family and other people forcefully to Bhulua. It was known as Bhulua Loot in folklore (Bhulua took by force).

The Khapura villagers informed the incidents to Chandradwip's King. The enraged king sent a letter to Manikya asking him to return his Kulaguru. Manikya replied, "Balak rajar eto spardha bhalo noy" (The boy-king must not be so audacious).

Furious, Ramchandra declared in the royal court, "Now Lakshman Manikya will witness the power of the boy-king." He ordered his generals to march to Bhulua. Among the five divisions of the army, they left one division to protect the capital Madhabpasha and four divisions were ordered to march to Kalyanpur. They crossed Kalijira River and surrounded Bhulua at night. The sound of cannons at night astonished Lakshman Manikya.

He fought bravely the next morning but was captured by the Ramchandra's army, who tied him with iron chains and took him to Chandradwip. Bhulua army fled in confusion. Raja Udaya Narayan, Lakshman Manikya's paternal uncle and elder son of King Rajballv Roy, was killed in the war.

The war was known as the Bakla war. A special court was summoned in the capital of Chandradwip. It gave a verdict that the Bhulua king should be hanged. But Ramchandra's mother advised him not to do so. Hence, Manikya was imprisoned. Once King Ramchandra was massaging oil before a bath and talking with others, Bhulua king was brought before him on his mother's advice. The Bhulua king put his weight on a coconut tree, and it fell near Ramchandra. Seeing this, his mother ordered the guards to kill Manikya. The guards beheaded the Bhulua king.

Another version about the death of Lakshman Manikya was that he was killed during the war against Magh pirates of Arakan in the year 1605 at Sandwip Island while he fought with other Kings against Magh pirates. But according to Pyarimohan Sen, author of the 'History of the Noakhali', Raja Ramchandra invited Raja Lakshman Manikya at his capital and murdered him by an assassination squad during a Boat safari. But the first version was more popular with the older generation than the other version.

Islam Khan was appointed the Subedar of Bengal in 1608 by the Mughal emperor Jahangir (1606-1627). He ruled Bengal from Jahangir Nagar, the old name of Dhaka. His major task was to control the rebellious Baro Bhuyan and Afgan Chief. He defeated Musa Khan, Pratapaditya of Jessore, Ram Chandra of Bakla, and Amar Manikya of Bhulua.

Amar Manikya, the eldest son of Raja Lakshman Manikya, became the king of Bhulua in 1609 A. D after the death of his father. He fought with the Mughal army and defeated at the hand of Subedar Islam Khan by the end of 1611 and fled to Arakan.

He thereafter ruled the Kalyanpur -Bhulua accepting the feudatory of Mughal Emperor **up to 1650 A.D**. With Lakshman Manikya, the royal line of independent Sur kings ended. But the descendants of Biswambhar Sur lived and ruled the Bhulua as a vassal of the Mughal Subedar and later the British East India Company.

On the Kalyanpur side, the last king was Raja Rudra Manikya, son of Amar Manikya, a 10th decedent of the founder king. **He ruled the Kalyanpur branch of Bhulua from 1650 to 1704 A.D**. He had no child. After his death, his widow, Rani Shashimukhi became ruler of the kingdom. She was the first female ruler of the Sur dynasty. **She ruled from 1704 to 1725 A.D**. After that; she left Bhulua and lived out her life in Kashi. During his rule, the Kalyanpur part of

Bhulua became fragmented. Royal employees of the Queen and different heads of Sur clan took Zamindary directly from Mughal Subedar, and they established different small Zamindaries at the Kalyanpur part of Bhulua. They paid revenue to the Mughal Subedar directly for their Zamindari estates. The new Zamindars were ruthless to collect taxes from their subjects.

Today, affluent persons are taxed to ease the poverty and hunger of the masses. But throughout history, Kings and Zamindars paid no tax, and instead, they taxed the poor peasantries to support their expensive wars and lifestyles. Peasantry paid tax despite poor harvest or drought, according to the demand of Zamindars who gave part of the collection to Kings or Sultanates or British Governor. Peasants survived in normal monsoons but died like flies during floods.

In the Zamindar system, Zamindars held enormous tracts of land and control over their peasants, from whom they reserved the right to collect the tax. So, the peasants were subjected to routine oppression by the Zamindar and his employees.

Zamindars used their lathiyals (muscular man equipped with cane) and private army to loot other Zamindar's estates. Some Zamindars kept their eyes closed to river pirates who operated in their Zamindari territories while they shared the loot and honoured the pirate heroes. Some Zamindars acted as a river pirate and attacked boats passing through their territories and looted valuables from the passenger of the boats.

There was an interesting story about a Zamindar pirate. A Zamindar pirate pirated a boat on the Meghna River at night and observed in the morning that it was his son-in-law's boat and his son-in-law was killed in scuffles with his men under cover of darkness.

As the Bhulua under the Kalyanpur part was divided into so many small Zamindaris, Rani Shashimukhi moved the temple of Goddess Barahi from Kalyanpur to the Amanishapara village with the help of the Royal head priest, Radha Kanta Chakraborty. The queen built a new temple in the Amanishapara and donated land in the name of the Maa Barahi to meet the recurring expenses of the temple.

Srirampur Branch of the Bhulu's Roy Families

Raja Krishna Chandra Roy, the elder son of King Kabichandra Khan, settled in Srirampur Rajbari (Srirampur Royal House) after the bifurcation of the Bhulua Kingdom. He was the founding father of the Srirampur branch of the Bhulua royal family. During his reign, Srirampur, his capital, came to prominence. He was a religious man and devoted much of his time to spiritual pursuits. Descendants of Raja Krishna Chandra Roy were not as industrious as his younger brother's descendants who settled at Kalyanpur. They were not effective and ruthless to collect revenue from their subjects. As a result, many times, they defaulted to pay revenues to Bengal Sultanate, Mughal Subahdar of Bengal, and at last East India Company. Tax from the land was a major source of revenue or income for the Sultans, emperors, and later the British East India Company.

The king levied a tax from his subject and used the taxes for the development and maintenance of the kingdom and gave part of the revenue to the Sultanates or Subedar or British. The Srirampur side collected it depending on the harvest of the crop. Floods were more or less a recurring phenomenon in Bhulua, and it was a major cause of crop damage. So, Kings of the Srirampur branch of the Bhulua were not ruthless to collect taxes from their subjects. They had traditions of showing some consideration to their tenants.

So, the Srirampur branch was punished for overdue land taxes, and their estate was auctioned for recovery of the default revenues several times. For that reason, they become ordinary public after 1833 when their last vestige of holdings was auctioned to recover overdue land revenue by the East India Company.

Bhulua was one of the major salts-producing centre of Bengal, which was run under the English salt agents. The British East India Company monopolised the salt production and salt trading business in Bengal. They paid royalties to the Srirampur Rajbari for their salt business in Bhulua. In 1821, Mr Plyden, the then British salt agent, got an additional charge of Collectorate of Bhulua from the Governor-General. Srirampur royal families were lazy and did not collect their royalties from Plyden and other Salt agents of Bhulua. They were busy with their other works. They thought the East India Company adjusted its arrear land revenues with their arrear royalties of salt, but it did not happen. The company auctioned their estate to recover the arrears land revenues without paying their arrears salt royalties.

The Decline of Srirampur branch of the Sur Dynasty

Bhulua covered an area of 635.85 sq km, paying the total land revenue of Rs 1, 23,929. In the Revenue settlement of 1728, part of Bhulua was recorded in the name of Raja Kriti Narayan, the last king of Srirampur side and 5th generations of the Raja Krishna Chandra Roy and 10th descendants of the founding father of Bhulua. In 1788, Mughal Subedar auctioned 4 Annas shares of the Bhulua Pargana recorded in the name of Raja Kriti Narayan Roy to recover the default revenue. Ganga Govinda Singha, owner of the royal house of Kandi at Murshidabad, and a resident of Paik para in Calcutta, purchased the properties. In 1833, the rest of the holding of the Srirampur king went to the auction to recover the arrear taxes of Zamindary by the agent of the East India Company. Dwarkanath Tagore, the grandfather of famous Bengali Nobel laureate poet Rabindra Nath Tagore, bought the remaining estate and sold it at Rs.3 lakhs to Rani Katyayani, widow of Krishna Chandra Sinha, better known as Lala Babu.

Indian moneyed classes were keen to buy Zamindary and became Zamindar in the absence of other effective outlets for investment. Ganga Govinda Singha was a revenue administrator of Bengal under Warren Hastings, the first Governor of Bengal, and he accumulated an immense fortune which enabled him to purchase Zamindary.

Arun Kumar Sinha, a descendant of Rani Katyayani and a member of the new Zamindar family of Noakhali, become president of Noakhali Sammilani, founded in 1905 in Calcutta and had been in office as president for 30 years.

Family Tree of Srirampur Branch of Sur (Roy) Dynasty

Raja Krishna Chandra Roy, the founder father of Srirampur's side, had two sons, elder, Raja Rup Narayan, and younger, Raja Barahi. **Elder Rup Narayan became king after the death of Krish Chandra Roy.**

King Rup Narayan had no children, **Kangsha Narayan, the eldest son of a younger brother Raja Barahi became King** of Srirampur side of the Bhulua kingdom after the death of Raja Rup Narayan.

Raja Kangsha Narayan also had two sons, elder Uday Narayan Manikya and younger Raja Chandra Narayan. **The elder son Raja Uday Narayan ascended the throne after the death of King Raja Kangsha Narayan.** Raja Uday Narayan ruled the Srirampur part of **Bhulua from 1725 to 1760** AD.

Raja Uday Narayan had three sons, the elder son who was the first in line to the throne was murdered, and so younger son **Raja Kriti Narayan became king after the death of King Raja Uday Narayan. Raja Kriti Narayan Roy ruled Bhulua from 1760 to 1788 A D.**

As stated before, during the regime of Raja Kriti Narayan, the largest holding of the kingdom was auctioned by Wazir to recover arrear land revenue of the estate in 1788 A D which was overdue to Mughal Subedar.

Raja Kriti Narayan, the last King of Bhulua from Srirampur's side, had four sons; Bhubaneswar Narayan was the eldest son. He had four sons. **Raja Raj Narayan** was one among the four sons of Bhubaneswar. **Raja Raj Narayan held the remaining smallholding from 1788 to 1833 A. D.**

In 1833, the rest of the estates of the Srirampur King that were put to auction for recovering arrears of land revenues by the East India Company. Rani Katyayani bought the holding via Prince Dwarkanath Tagore. The first few decades of British rules saw the rigid law of revenue collection under which, in case of delay in payment, the Zamindary estates were sold to the highest bidder to recover overdue revenue.

Chandra Narayan was the only son of Raja Raj Narayan. Chandra Narayan had two sons, the elder, Lakhi Narayan, and the younger, Golak Narayan. Lakhi Narayan had an immense influence over the Union Board, and he was also president of Ramganj High School.

Lakhi Narayan had two sons, the elder, Nagendra Narayan, and younger, Girindra Narayan. The elder Nagendra Narayan **had three sons, Birendra, Sailendra, and Khagendra.** The younger Girindra Narayan had no children.

Raja Nagendra Narayan and his extended family were a rioters target during the pro-Pakistan riots, as they were descendants of the Hindu Kings. A Muslim mob stormed the Srirampur Rajbari and they looted belongings and burned the house. Law enforcement agencies did not protect the residents during the pre and post riots periods. Although the massacre and the conversion stopped in November 1946, normalcy was never restored until the partition.

The partition had left 40 million Muslims in India. The bulk of them had, under the Muslim League's propaganda, given their active or passive support to the partition of India. The leaders had migrated to Pakistan, leaving their supporters in a real quandary. They felt disillusioned.

Monitoring the ancestry of the royal families with different branches is difficult for the reader, so I give below the Family tree of the Sur dynasty starting from its founder to the last generation who fled from Noakhali because of atrocities committed against them.

Family tree of the Bhulua royal family
(Ancestry chart)

1. *Raja Biswambhar Sur, founder King of the Bhulua Pargana, Ruled 1203–1250AD, Capital–Kalyanpur, his descendants ruled the independent Bhulua Pargana, the next 400 years.*

2. *After his demise, his elder son, Ganapati Ray became King, Ruled 1250–1300 AD.*

3. *Next King Raja Shurananda Khan, the only son of Ganapati, Ruled 1300–1345 AD.*

4. *Raja Sriram Khan, elder son of Shurananda Khan, next King, Ruled 1345–1410, Srirampur village, and Srirampur Royal Palace or fort were built during his rule.*

5. *Raja Kabi Chandra Khan, the only son of Sriram, next King, Rule 1410–1470 AD. He had two sons; they divided the Bhulua Kingdom into two parts and ruled separately.*

6. **Elder, Raja Krishna Chandra Roy, settled at Srirampur Rajbari. Founder father of Srirampur Branch of Bhulua, he had two sons.**

6) Younger, Raja Rajbalav Roy settled at Kalyanpur, Founder of Kalyanpur Branch of Bhulua, he had two sons.

Krishna Chandra Roy

7. **1) Rup Narayan**   **2) Barahi**
   Have no child   *two sons*

8. **1) Kansa Narayan**   **2) Nara Narayan**
   Two sons have   no children

9. **1) Udaya Narayan**   **2) Chandra Narayan**
   Three sons   No child

10. **1. Rup**   **2. Pratap.**   **3. Kriti Narayan**
    1. Murdered 2. No child   3. Four sons

11. **1. Bhubaneshwar**   **2. Raghunath**   **3. Krishna**   **4. Rajkrishna.**
    Four sons   No child   No child   No child

12. **1. Raj Narayan**   **2. Bir Narayan**   **3. Sur Narayan 4. Rajkishore**
    One son   *No child*   *Two sons*   *No child.*

Raja Rajbalav Roy

1) Udaya Narayan   2) Gandharba Manikha
Have no child   *two sons*

1) Ananta   2) Lakshman Manikya.
No child.   Four sons

1) Amar   2)Brama   3) Joy   4) Chandra
1) Rudra   2) No child   3) Ram 4) No child
Rudra was the next King, he had no child, after his
death, Rani Shashimukhi ruled the Kalayanpur Bhulua.

13. **Chandra Narayan**   **1. Gour 2. Bhirab.**
    Two sons   *No information*

14. **1. Lakshmi Narayan Roy**   **2. Golak Narayan Roy.**
    Two sons   *No information*

15. **1. Nagendra Narayan Roy.**   **2. Girindra Narayan Roy.**
    Three Sons   *No child*

16. **1. Birendra**   **2. Sailendra**   **3. Khagendra.**
    Five sons   Three sons   Two sons.
    I   I   I
    wife- Parul   *wife- Ava*   *wife-Biva, elder son-Chandan*

"If you don't know history, you don't know anything.
You are a leaf that doesn't know it is part of a tree."

– Michael Crichton

Nagendra's Family

Khagendra was a youthful man when Mahatma Gandhi camped in their house at Srirampur Rajbari. He was the youngest son of Raja Nagendra Narayan and the 4th descendant of the last King of Raja Kriti Narayan. They were no more Kings, but used to live in an extended family in their ancestral royal palace at Srirampur and led a very simple and humble life. There were several children in the joint family of the Rajbari but Khagendra was a pampered kid among children as he used to sing Kirtan (a devotional song about the life of Krishna) at a family's Durga Dalan (permanent building for Durga Puja) in the evening after school hour.

In Sur family, auspicious pitcher or Mangal Ghat was used as a Durga, instead of a Durga idol. It was said that once, a minor girl disappeared from the Puja Dalan or Durga temple during Durga Puja at Rajbari, later her saree was found in the mouth of the Durga's lion. After that, they performed Durga Puja using Gold plated Mangal Kalash or an auspicious pitcher made of gold.

A nationalistic atmosphere prevailed in Rajbari as it prevailed in the days of their forefathers who had defied the Muslim conquers centuries ago and set up independent principalities in Bengal.

Khagendra's elder brother Birendra was an active participant in the Independence movement and joined as a worker of a secret revolutionary terrorist group at an early age. He often remained absent from the house and bunked off school for Swadeshi activities. Sometimes, he abstained from the school examination but appeared after the persuasion of the elders. At 15, he became the youngest matriculate in the Noakhali and passed with flying colours. After matriculation, he engaged in the freedom struggle and worked full time for revolutionary activities. He was arrested for revolutionary activities by Daroga of local Thana. Police detained him in the police station and brutally tortured during the interrogation. They brought handcuffed Birendra from Noakhali to Chittagong. He was imprisoned in Chittagong Central Jail for several years without a proper trial. He did not give an undertaking, as suggested by British Warden, pledging his loyalty to the British Government in return for being released from prison. They released him from jail before the Noakhali riots.

There was no college at Noakhali. Khagendra went to Calcutta for further study after matriculation. He stayed as a tutor in the house of Mahendra Nath Ghosh, an Advocate of Calcutta High Court, Vice President of Noakhali Sammilani and Hindu Mahasabha, and a relative of the family. He passed Intermediate Examination from South Suburban College, now Asutosh College, and completed B. Sc with distinction from St Xavier's College in Calcutta. He returned to Srirampur after his bachelor's degree before

Noakhali carnage and engaged as a Village School Master in a Ramganj Madhupur High School at Ramganj.

During peace missions to riot-hit areas, Gandhi set up his base in a half-burnt Srirampur Rajbari and occupied a spacious hut in the centre of a courtyard surrounded by coconut and betelnut trees. There were other several huts nearby. Few huts of the royal palace were completely burned during the Noakhali riots. A Muslim boy who looked after the cows led rowdies to attack and set fire to the house. Several large tanks were there within the compound. Residents of the Rajbari left the house during the riots but returned after Gandhi's arrival. Khagendra's mother and wife of Nripen Raja prepared breakfast, lunch, and dinner for Mahatma according to Mahatma's choice and availability of vegetables at Srirampur. On 23-11-1946, Gandhiji ate Sponge gourd (dhundul), a local vegetable, and fell sick. The climate of Noakhali was damp, and the soil remained wet even in December. It was difficult for Gandhiji to cope up with the damp climate of East Bengal.

Khagendra was influenced by Mahatma's ideology & simple life and wrote a book about Gandhiji, but it was not published. Mr Nirmal Kumar Bose, a leading anthropologist, and director of the Anthropological Survey of India worked as a secretary and an interpreter of Gandhiji during his peace mission in Noakhali. Gandhi Maharaj, as stated by Nirmal Kumar Bose, lived a very simple life and his day began at 4 a.m. and everything went according to plan throughout the day. Sarojini Naidu joked once "To keep Mahatma Gandhi poor, we have to destroy treasures. His poverty is very costly." Gandhiji's detailed day-to-day life in Srirampur Rajbari was described by Mr Nirmal Kumar Bose in his book "My Days with Gandhi." Prof. Nirmal Kumar Bose described the inhabitants of Rajbari in the book as "the inmates belonged to one of the most ancient and respectable families of Noakhali. They were descended from one of the twelve feudal chiefs who had successfully defied the Muslim conquers centuries ago and set up an independent principality in Bengal." The members of the family actively took part in the freedom movement for which the British Government arrested and imprisoned some members.

Many leaders, both from Hindu and Muslim communities came to Gandhiji and discussed so many things about communal harmony, peace, non-violence and ways and means to implement it in riot-affected areas, but that did not work. According to Ashoka Gupta, "The word of peace remained confined to Gandhiji and a handful of his followers. In the daily prayer meetings, his words of peace did not draw takers. He realized how futile it all was. He was a lonely man, in deep pain and helplessness."

In this regard, Gandhi made an important clarification in a letter he wrote from Srirampur: "I am certain that the principle of truth and non-violence can never be wrong or defective; but this case (of Noakhali) may show up the deficiency of its exponent and avowed representative, i.e., myself. If that is so, I only hope that God will be merciful enough to call me back to Him and get His work done through a worthier soul."

Madhu Dandwate said in a lecture. "There were 'brave men' in India who from housetops were saying: "Hindus are being butchered, they are subjected to atrocities in Noakhali and we must save them." But, there was only one Gandhi and his peace mission went to Noakhali."

Assimilation of Kalyanpur into Srirampur Branch

Before the Noakhali genocide, as stated earlier, Khagendra worked as a schoolteacher in a nearby school. After the Noakhali riots, he stopped to go to that school in the Muslim dominated locality and tried to get another job. He got a Sub Inspector job in Police but his parents did not allow him to join the British Government's police force. He got married just before the Noakhali genocide to Biva, a descent from the royal families of the Kalyanpur branch. Biva lost her mother when she was just 6 months old, and her father did not marry again. She was brought up by Charubala, wife of the elder brother of Biva's father, along with her own family. Biva's father lived with his elder brother's family in old Noakhali town, and Charubala raised Biva like a mother. The elder brother of Biva's father was a Railway Station Master, and they were descendants of the Raja Lakshman Manikya of Kalyanpur's side. Charubala was from the **Srirampur** side and the elder sister of Khagendra. The ancestral house of Kalyanpur Rajbari vanished in the Meghna River long back.

Biva's father was a lawyer at Noakhali District Civil Court, and he was busy with his legal profession. In Noakhali, the continued deposition of silt in the Meghna River formed sizable new land or Char in the river. It was valuable land for agricultural purposes. Influential people grabbed this newly formed land with the help of lathiyals (Strong man equipped with cane) and a lawyer. Biva's father helped others as a lawyer to capture the Char lands.

He returned home late at night. Biva stayed alone in his room and waited for her father. Her father brought fancy foods, which they shared in their room.

Her demeanour was self-effacing, but she was a lovely and gracious woman.

She was not accustomed to the household chores of cooking, cleaning, and doing laundry, as there was a household staff that took care of these works. She faced problems at her father-in-law's house after marriage. During her pre-marriage days, she was pleasant, but a shy, bookish type and kept herself busy with romantic literature and Sarat Babu's novels which she collected from the Noakhali District Library. Biva's secluded life and bookish habits made her a dreamer just opposite to her practical husband who did not have a romantic bone in his body. Khagendra was raised in a household where displays of any emotion were discouraged. Biva's romance fizzled out after a few months of her marriage.

She encountered Khagendra, younger brother of her Charubala auntie, a couple of times before her engagement as the family members of the Srirampur Rajbari took part in the Kalyanpur royal family's wedding or other ceremonies because of their family relations. Biva developed a crush on aunty's younger brother, who was then a graduate student at Calcutta University.

Bava's father liked Khagendra, considering the histories of the royals where marriage within relation was ideal to keep the body-line strong. Charubala auntie also thought Biva would be happy in her father's house if she got married to her younger brother. Her father, understanding his daughter's and sister-in -law's feelings, but worried about her age, waited until Biva was 16. So the two got engaged by the summer of 1946, by common consent of all concerned when Biva was about 16 years old and Khagendra was then a schoolteacher.

We considered Marriage a cultural universal. In some form or another, we found it worldwide across all cultures. At the very beginning of their marriage, Biva faced a hard practical adult life, dissimilar from her bookish world. She was busy with her duties as a newlywed bride in her in law's extended joint family. She understood actual life was not like fairy tales wherein Cinderella found her prince and lived happily thereafter.

She moved her in-laws' house after being matriculated and could not continue further study because of her marriage and riots. After the Noakhali carnage, when family members preparing to leave the Noakhali, she lugged her books and carried it. She was an avid reader of novels throughout her life.

"We, unaccustomed to courage
exiles from delight
live coiled in shells of loneliness
until love leaves its high holy temple
and comes into our sight
to liberate us into life.
We are weaned from our timidity
In the flush of love's light
We dare be brave
And suddenly we see
that love costs all we are
and will ever be.
Yet it is only loved
This sets us free."

– By Maya Angelou

Partition Woes

Biva had a stillborn daughter after the violence of the Noakhali riots. It was a time when women's plight was worst of all. They had to watch their husbands being murdered and then be forcibly converted and married to those responsible for their death. The Rajbari's family was in grave danger. The Srirampur Rajbari was on fire during the riot. One house was completely gone and another one was partially damaged. The fire was started by a Muslim boy whose family worked in the Royal Palace at least three generations. Muslim rioters plundered their house. The inmates, during the communal disturbance, had taken shelter elsewhere, but when Gandhiji came and settled down in their half-burnt house, they returned to their home. Suspicion and insecurity were so deep among inmates; it did not put an end, despite Gandhi in their house. After the departure of Gandhi from Noakhali, communal flare-up was re-escalated in Srirampur. Inmates of the Rajbari decided to abandon the Noakhali for the safety and security of the members. In the morning, Nagendra Narayan Roy left the Srirampur Rajbari by the back door with his wife and other family members. Not long after they moved, tragedy struck, Nagendra Narayan suffered from cholera on the way and died at the Chandpur launch Terminal. Thousands of refugees left Noakhali daily on ferries. The Roy family packed with other refugees shoulder to shoulder on the launch. The death of the head of the family at the time of fleeing towards the Indian border caused unbearable pain and emotional turmoil to the rest of the family members, but they did not have the opportunity and luxury to grieve for their family head's death. They, along with thousands of refugees, moved towards the border. Despite mishaps, they crossed the border. Sailendra, the second son of Nagendra, who lived in Calcutta, went to Petrapole (Indian side of the border with erstwhile East Pakistan) to receive the family. When he saw his mother in a widow's dress, he broke down and cried.

**When we left
the night was blue
the moon not full
A path
to where?
to here
choices made**

of what was lost
Look back
the distant light
of faded hope
lingering pain's
what's left to hold
When we left
in the blue of a night
with a crescent moon
light the sky.

– By Cynthia Richards

The royal refugee family took shelter first in a relative house at the Howrah Rail Colony; thereafter, they rented a small house at Dum Dum, a suburb of Calcutta, where all the members of the extended family were forced to live in a cramped space. The areas were crowded and filthy. Life in the unknown place was unfulfilling and joyless.

Only one member of the family had a job in Calcutta who came to this part of Bengal long before the Noakhali carnage, and he lived in a workingman's mess in Calcutta. The Khagendra's mother could not reconcile with the sudden, drastic, horrible changes in her life. She stopped talking and worked silently with a blank, emotionless eye. Other members also had a dead look at the rapidly changing situation they underwent within a few months.

Khagendra got a temporary job at a refugee rehabilitation department of the Govt of West Bengal. All refugees were facing umpteenth problems after fleeing from East Pakistan as there were no food, shelter, and rehabilitation program for traumatized refugees in West Bengal.

The most troublesome problem of the Govt was to face the continuous influx of refugees that began in the aftermath of partition and continued thereafter for decades. Local and central governments were confused and indifferent towards refugees' rehabilitation. It was estimated that one million refugees crossed into West Bengal, particularly the aftermath of the Noakhali and Barisal riots. The majority settled in the city of Kolkata and its suburb. They were facing resistance from the local inhabitants as they occupied all vacant lands in and around Calcutta. Landowners sent goons to evict the refugees and to vacate the lands occupied illegally by them. Bloody clashes between goons and refugees were a regular feature in and around Calcutta and its suburb. Refugees also put up resistance against landowners' attempts to evict them. Names like Bijoygarh and Azadgarh marked the success of the refugees in holding the 'fort. Local people called refugees as 'Bangal' means who were uncivilized and rustic as they made their areas congested and dirty. In 1950, there were 150 colonies in and around Calcutta. Squatters in the colony were in a way self-settles in the absence of official arrangements for rehabilitation.

Member of the former King's family of Srirampur had used Raja as a prefix before their name. But when the children of the family went to the local school to get admitted, the school advised them not to use Raja as a prefix in their name as Raja title debarred them from the refugee stipend in school. The family members of Srirampur Rajbari have not used the Raja title as a prefix to their name since then.

Despondent days were passing, they felt there was no hope, there was nothing left but deep down, they felt they would escape this.

"Extreme hopes are born of extreme misery"

– Bertrand Russell

At Dum Dum, Biva and other women in the family became very depressed in the unfamiliar environment, as, in this place, there were no trees, rivers, open fields, greenery as existed in the Noakhali and they lived now in ghetto conditions. Deep in Dumdum, people were living in terrible poverty in shacks. The Rajbari's refugees were forced to live in squalor. The privacy of the ladies was now an illusion. They used the pond for washing utensils and clothes, and also for bathing. Safe drinking water was also not available. Life became absolute hell. It was a horrible place as described in religious books where the evil soul was subjected to punitive suffering.

'Home'

"No one leaves home unless
home is the mouth of a shark
you only run for the border
when you see the whole city running as well.
No one leaves home until the home is a sweaty
voice in your ear

saying-

leave

run away from me now
I don't know what I've become
but I know that anywhere
is safer than here."

— Few Stanzas from 'Home' by Warsan Shire

Pritilata Waddedar (5 May1911-23 September 1932) was a school teacher, joined a revolutionary group headed by Surya Sen. She was among the initial lot of revolutionary who picked up arms against the British Raj and led an armed attack on the European Club in Chittagong. She was Bengal's First Woman Martyr, who died then be caught by the British.

Some Thoughts about Refugees and Pre and Post-Independent India

It was a great irony that 2.6 million Hindus, according to the 1951 census, moved from East Bengal to West Bengal and massive violence and slaughter had occurred with the death of so many refugees. It did not get due recognition in Indian history in post-independence India. The history books are filled up with a few names. They wrote a distorted history of India's freedom struggle and recorded a one-sided picture of the freedom movement, only emphasized on a handful of national leaders, but it was a mass movement of peasants, workers, and lower middle class who came out on the street in a million.

The fundamental lesson of history is ' The week will be killed; the strong would not mention it when they write history." Perhaps that is the reason that Noakhali riots are not mentioned in our history books.

After independence, there were no trials or commission took place, or they filed no charges against those who supported genocide and ethnic cleansing as happened in countries in Yugoslavia, or Cambodia. There was no "Truth and Reconciliation Commission" as happened in post-apartheid South Africa. If you read India's freedom struggle, you learned that two men mattered in India's freedom, Gandhi and Nehru. The rest was just appendages. The sacrifice of thousands of freedom fighters, revolutionaries, people killed because of religion-based partition, refugees who faced prolong and widespread suffering, sacrifices of the ordinary peoples' and significant contribution of INA fighters (6000 INA fighters sacrificed their lives in Imphal-Kohima borders) have not got due importance and recognition in India's independence history.

How we forgot the various tribal rebellions and peasant uprisings during British rule before Indian independence. The Royal Indian Navy revolt at Bombay Harbour on 18 Feb 1946 against Colonial rule was seen as an event making the end of British Rule. We now see, a Political Party takes credit for independence and they boast that they sacrificed lots in the Indian freedom movement and negated the sacrifice of millions of others. Builders of Modern India, according to Government of India, Department of the post (DOP) was only five Indian individuals beside Gandhi and B. R. Ambedkar, they were Nehru, Indira, and Rajiv Gandhi for postal release launched by the Dept of Post on 1st December 2008. After independence, everything, roads, airports, stadiums, government projects, educational institutes, and so on named after a few. Other than a few politicians, nobody in our vast country has got an acknowledgement in public life.

More than a thousand Zamindari estates and Jagirs along with the 565 princely states realized that they owed their existence because of British rule and always wanted to maintain the colonial rules. The Zamindars and ruling royalties were the loyal supporters of the British government. After independence, they become Chief Minister, central Minister, or MLA or MP in our independent country.

This awful chapter in Indian history as violent as of Partition and the largest forced migration of human, unheard of in Europe and America, and the rest of the world for the independence of a country. It violated fundamental human rights. European countries had colonies throughout the world. The colonial ruler looted the colony under their possession and enriched their own country. The well planned modern European cities were made from the plundered wealth of their occupied territories. Western countries are talking about Human rights and passed "the bill of Right" in long back in their country, but they were the worst violator of Human rights in their colonies.

British India oppressed, killed, tortured, and maimed the inhabitant of the Indian Subcontinent for 200 years. The colonial ruler ruled the Indian Subcontinent by dividing and ruling policy, by creating or encouraging divisions among the subjects to prevent alliances that could challenge their sovereign. They aided and promoted those who cooperated with the Colonial Ruler and fostered distrust and enmity between local rulers, a different religion, and different communities.

The seeds of mistrust and enmity between Hindu and Muslim, both of whom coexisted for several centuries-long as a big family, were encouraged and they succeeded to create two countries in the Indian Subcontinent by partitioning

British India and partitioned halves are engaged in a bloody war and acrimony since independence.

India, before the British, was a wealthy country accounted for 25% of global GDP and was very poor and backward once when they left. Wages and living standards in Mughal India were even higher than England, which had the best standard of living in Europe.

Netaji Subhas Chandra Bose advocated complete, unconditional independence for India, not independence with partition. He vanished in the cloud, and it was assumed that the Taihoku plane crash on 18th Aug 1945 was a planted story. He became a threat to political leaders of pre-independent India as they sought to keep their hegemony on the Indian National Congress and the independence movements of Pre-Independent India. They snooped the Netaji family also after independence for 20 years.

Netaji's daughter, Mrs Anita Bose Pfaff in an interview told, "My father resigned as Congress president in the1930, Gandhi worked against him. Often Gandhi is portrayed as a saint, which he was not at all. In my opinion, he was a very shrewd politician. He was a lawyer who knew how to work the system and manipulate people in a positive sense. He certainly made my father resigned as Congress president."

British Prime Minister Clement Attlee had himself agreed that "Subhas Chandra Bose played a key role in triggering the feeling of nationalism and revolt among the soldiers of the British Indian Army. As more and more people joined the INA and the way the Indian National

Army (INA) was ready to fight against the British, it was a signal that they won't be able to hold India and it was the main cause that the British were forced to leave India."

The role of the INA in the country's independence struggle has been obliterated from history.

Alexander the Great might just be right: "I am not afraid of an army of lions led by a sheep; I am afraid of an army of sheep led by a lion." The leadership of Bose, like a lion, was a cause for significant concern for the British and others.

- Achintya Kumar Sengupta, son of Noakhali, wrote a Bengali poem about the feeling of ordinary Bengali, one lived under Pakistan and other under India, both come from similar backgrounds, speak the same language, have the same cultural traditions and artistic heritage, but partitioned on the religious line as demanded as a pre-condition of independence which was/is unheard of anywhere in the world.

পুব-পশ্চিম

অচিন্ত্যকুমার সেনগুপ্ত

তোমার শীতললক্ষ্যা আর আমার ময়ূরাক্ষী
তোমার ভৈরব আর আমার রূপনারায়ণ
তোমার কর্ণফুলি আর আমার শিলাবতী
তোমার পায়রা আর আমার পিয়ালী
এক জল এক ঢেউ এক ধারা
একই শীতল অতল অবগাহন, শুভদায়িনী শান্তি।
তোমার চোখের আকাশের রোদ আমার চোখের উঠোনে
          এসে পড়ে
তোমার ভাবনার বাতাস আমার ভাবনার বাগানে ফুল
          ফোটায়।

তোমার নারকেল সুপুরি অশোক শিমুল
আমার তাল খেজুর শাল মহুয়া
এক ছায়া এক মায়া একই মুকুল মঞ্জরী।
তোমার ভাটিয়াল আমার গম্ভীরা
তোমার সারি-জারি আমার বাউল
এক সুর এক টান একই অকূলের আকৃতি
তোমার টাঙ্গাইল আমার ধনেখালি
তোমার জামদানি আমার বালুচর
এক সুতো এক ছন্দ একই লাণেয়র টানা-পোড়েন
চলেছে একই রূপনগরের হাতছানিতে।

আমরা এক বৃন্তে দুই ফুল, এক মাঠে দুই ফসল
আমাদের খাঁচার ভিতরে একই অচিন পাখির আনাগোনা।
আমার দেবতার থানে তুমি বটের ঝুরিতে সুতো বাঁধো
আমি তোমার পীরের দরগায় চেরাগ জ্বালি।
আমার সেতাতরপাঠ তোমাকে ডাকে
তোমার আজান আমাকে খুঁজে বেড়ায়।

আমাদের এক সুখ এক কান্না এত পিপাসা
ভূগোল ইতিহাসে আমরা এক
এক মন এক মানুষ এক মাটি এক মমতা
পরস্পর আমরা পর নই
আমরা পড়শী---আর পড়শীই তো আরশি
তুমি সুলতানা আমি অপূর্ব
আমি মহবুব তুমি শ্যামলী।

আমাদের শত্রুও সেই এক
যারা আমাদের আস্ত মস্ত সোনার দেশকে খন্ড-খন্ড
        করেছে
যারা আমাদের রাখতে চায় বিচ্ছিন্ন করে বিরূপ করে বিমুখ করে
        ।
কিন্তু নদীর দুর্বার জলকে কে বাঁধবে
কে রুখবে বাতাসের অবাধ স্রোত
কে মুছে দেবে আমাদের মুখের ভাষা আমাদের রক্তের
        কবিতা
আমাদের হৃদয়ের গভীর গুঞ্জন?
তুমি আমার ভাষা বলো আমি আনন্দকে দেখি
আমি তোমাদের ভাষা বলি তুমি আশ্চর্যের দেখ
এই ভাষায় আমাদের আনন্দ -আশ্চর্যের সাক্ষাত্কার।
কার সাধ্য অমৃতদীপিত সূর্য-চন্দ্রকে কেড়ে নেবে
        আকাশ থেকে?

আমাদের এক রবীন্দ্রনাথ এক নজরুল।
আমরা ভাষায় এক ভালোবাসায় এক মানবতায় এক
বিনা সুতোয় রাখীবন্ধনের কারিগর
আমরাই একে অন্যের হৃদয়ের অনুবাদ
অমরের মধুকর, মঙ্গলের দূত
আমরাই চিরন্তন কুশলসাধক ||

The Condition of the Rajbari's Refugees

There is an old saying "What does not kill you, strengthen you."

Family members, under the changed situation, led a tough life and were busy to get the basic needs. During that crucial period, Khagendra lost his temporary job. He started a job search, but there was no job. The Displaced person from East Pakistan concentrated in the city of Calcutta and everybody needed a job for livelihood. All refugees struggled to find a job, and getting a job was like winning a lottery.

"No man has hired us
With pocketed hands
And lowered faces
We stand about in open places.
And shiver in unlit rooms."

– By T. S. Eliot

Not finding a job, Khagendra started a toilet soap manufacturing unit. The name of the soap was Champion. But the poor marketability of the toilet shop drove the small farms out of business. The soap became hard in winter, but soft in the summer. He raised his start-up capital for the unit by selling his wife's ornaments.

After the failure of his first endeavour, he sold the remaining jewellery of Biva and started a Packaging box manufacturing business at Ultadanga near Calcutta.

He supplied his products to the Burrabazar Wholesale Market in Calcutta on trade credit but did not get payment from them. He shut the unit down because of a lack of capital. Then he, at last, started a grocery shop, but it also did not work as he could not invest more cash. After a business failure, he felt very upset. Everything he had worked for was gone and to make matters worse, he lost his confidence too.

The Ordnance Factory Board recruited graduate apprentices in a regular interval for technical jobs. Khagendra did not want to leave Kolkata and wanted to stay with the family as the family was in crisis. Losing hope to get a job in Bengal, he applied for the graduate apprentice job. Being selected, he joined in the 3rd batch as a graduate trainee in the year 1949 at the Katni Ordnance Factory, Madhya Pradesh, and gave bond, not to leave Ordnance within 5 years after completion of the training. At the end of the training, the Board posted him in the Ambarnath ordnance factory near Kalyan in Maharashtra as a technical supervisor.

Biva stayed on at Dumdum with her in-laws. They were used to having a different lifestyle and status in Noakhali, so it took a while for them to adjust to the present condition. She became the mother of a boy child in Dumdum, and the baby's name was Chandan. Biva suffered post-delivery complications (Sutika disease) after childbirth. Parul, the wife of Khagendra's elder brother, took care of Biva as she remained sick for a few months.

Chandan was born and brought up in hard times when the family could not afford the expenses of baby food or cow milk. He used to take wheat flour mixed with water as a substitute for milk, but the child had no problem drinking it. Biva thought Chandan deserved better treatment than this. He was always with a smile in a family, where everybody was serious to cope with the changed circumstances. The child had shown exceptional adaptability to difficult situations and helped seniors in their daily work. Sometimes, he made things unpleasant for family, mixed water with oil, sand with spices, ate cooked foods from the kitchen, and made food cooked for the widow inedible by mixing it with non-vegetarian foods. So, Chandan was always under the strict vigilance of elders. When he was two, he had a sister. The baby was a quiet girl. Chandan was curious about everything around him. He was so far an only child in the house. Now he was informed, God had given us a new baby girl. He looked at the recent arrival from head to toe and then said: "God can take her away again."

After a few initial turbulent years, Khagendra's brothers were scattered and settled in different places. The elder brother, Birendra, settled in the Baghajatin locality in Jadavpur. He worked at Jabalpur Cantonment Board, a defence organization. All of a sudden, he resigned from that service and joined a Gujarati farm in Calcutta. At an advanced age, he controlled his dying by making a conscious decision to refuse food and stopped talking. He did not want to go through any medical treatment, no hospitalization, and no ventilation. He always wanted a peaceful death at home. The practice of bringing about one's death by refusing to eat or drink is not new. In India, members of the Jain religion have practised Santhara for well over 2000 years.

The second brother, Sailendra, rented a house at Sitaram Ghosh Street in Calcutta and lived with their mother. He worked at the Punjab National Bank and joined Bank before the partition of British India. After a few years, he purchased a piece of land at Dumdum and built a house beside his elder sister, Charubala's house. Charubala died of pile's cancer in 1965. Khagendra's mother died a few years after the partition at Sitaram Ghosh Street, Calcutta. She never recovered from the trauma she went through during the Noakhali carnage. The bad incidences such as riots, rioters torched the house, and widowhood at the time of escape from Noakhali left a deep scar on her and she never healed from that trauma.

Khagendra took the family at Ambernath at his workplace when Chandan was three years old. They admitted Chandan to Fatima High School in west Ambernath. He used to go to school with other children in the neighbourhood. Biva used to get complaints that Chandan was doing mischief in school. In the beginning, they scolded Chandan, but later, they stopped to say anything. The Khagendra's family took daily foods together with Nirmal Choudhury, a bachelor office colleague of Khagendra and Raghavan, an Andhraite, an employee of Ordnance factory. Biva faced difficulties to manage the household chores along with bringing up her three children though Raghavan assisted her after his duty hour. In Ambernath, she saw a new culture where an official position of the husband at a working place determined the social position or status of the family in the Industrial Township.

Industrial Township was a class-conscious society. In a small town, everybody knew everybody. Privacy found in a metro city was missing here. Khagendra was busy with card games at the Bengali Club after office hours and played football on holiday. On a winter morning, Biva went to the Ambreshwar temple, an 11th-century Hindu temple on a hill at Ambernath, to worship Lord Shiva with Chandan along with other neighbours. When she was busy with the worship of Lord Shiva, she heard a loud noise from outside; she went out of the temple and informed by other worshipers that a boy jumped from the hill. Biva came down from the hill and saw that it was Chandan, and he could not move his arm. She took him to the Ordnance Hospital. The hospital X-rayed his affected parts. The doctor said viewing his X-ray plate, his collarbone was fractured. His fractured collarbone was then plastered. There was no scope to inform Khagendra. When Khagendra returned at night from the Bengali club after playing cards, he saw Chandan sat with a sling. Nirmalbabu said to Khagendra, why he came home every day late at night.

Biva felt depressed with the incidents happened one after another after her marriage, the death of her first child, Noakhali riots, Fire on their house and loot, Gandhiji's stay, visit of Jawaharlal Nehru and other bigwigs of Indian politics, then fleeing in haste to Calcutta, the birth of Chandan, hard post-partition days in Dum Dum and birth of a baby girl, shifting again to class-conscious Ambernath, the birth of another baby boy, rigorous household chores and so on, all these incidents in quick succession affected Biva and left a scar. When she was alone, she recalled her happy old days in Noakhali amid flora, fauna, and books.

> **Night dawns quick on the village**
> **Stars are drunk with the smell of earth**
> **Behind the cloud, the moon is a wispy haze**
> **Cricket cut the dark with cacophonous mirth.**
>
> **Here I was born I left my thread**
> **The damp earth knows the trail of my feet**
> **Uprooted time made me a city-bred**
> **in the wind here lingers long lost heartbeat.**
>
> **Upon the soil here echoes the unheard dewdrop**
> **Shadows huddle in the breath of starlight**
> **worried heads dream of golden crop**
> **chisel a world at the end of a long night.**
>
> **What if these moments plant me a seed?**
> **that sprouts to a wish long craving to be born**
> **I stay back here and wide-eyed read**
> **How dark sky fades into a blood sun morn.**
>
> **– Written by poetry journal, Oct 2015**

When the family was accustomed to the surroundings, Khagendra suddenly resigned from the Ordnance factory and left Ambernath before the completion of his service bond period.

"I hate getting flashbacks of things I do not want to remember. I also don't like the status-conscious society. I feel depressed."

– Quote from an unknown source

Chandan, a naughty boy with a big heart

Life After the Initial Hiccups

The family came back to Dum Dum at Bava's father's incomplete house. Khagendra joined the Sen-Raleigh cycle factory in Konyapur near Asansol, which came into existence in 1949 in collaboration with the Raleigh Cycle of Nottingham. They supplied the popular cycle to all parts of India and outside. The total workforce was more than a thousand who were employed directly or indirectly with the company. The factory was closed down in 2002.

Bava's father as a refugee did not get any brief as a lawyer in Calcutta Court. He, at last, applied and joined as a mathematics teacher in the Jadavpur High School. The salary of a high school teacher was then very meagre. He purchased a piece of land at Dum Dum in 1950 and constructed a small house on his purchased land. To get money for construction, he took house tuition job.

Widowed Charubala aunty purchased an adjacent land of Biva's father and built on it a one-room house. Biva lived with them until she shifted to Asansol. After a few months, Khagendra took his family to Asansol at his new workplace.

In Asansol, they admitted Chandan at Ramakrishna Mission High School. Here medium of teaching was

Bengali, since he had so far studied in English medium, Chandan faced difficulty. He performed poorly in the Annual Examination. Khagendra engaged a Bengali teacher for Chandan. Biva was always behind Chandan and reminded him that being a refugee, his future depends on education. Khagendra took a rented house at the Railpar in Asansol. In those days, Congress ruled both the states and country, but the trade union wing of the Communist Party of India influenced the industrial workers of Bengal.

As time passed, the refugees became disenchanted with the Congress Party and Congress Government in Bengal. Disappointment among the refugees turned bitter against the entire Congress establishment. Communist party engineered protest rally and demonstration using disenchanted people and refugees in Bengal. Many trade union leaders viewed entrepreneurs and managers as myopic vampires. This perception gave birth to discontent between management staff and labours.

Bengal was a developed province before independence. The decline of Bengal from its rosy days was because of the large influxes of refugees, militant trade unionism, freight equalization policy in 1952, pressure on land resources, absence of Industrial Modernisation, and industrial disputes, and so forth.

Khagendra saw high unemployment in Bengal at the same time *there was high militancy among workers and they were engaged in militant trade unionism in the industries.* Unemployed men of different ages came into his house seeking a job. Relatives urged him to give employment to their children. He tried his best to get them used. When the rush became unmanageable, he became indifferent.

Biva requested her husband on behalf of the unemployed to get them used as few of them stood in front of their house every evening. School days of Chandan in Asansol were a sheltered and uneventful one. In 1962, Khagendra tendered his resignation from the cycle Company in Asansol and joined a Govt. Undertaking in Durgapur.

Khagendra's new Employer was a Public Sector Undertaking (PSU) which was set up in collaboration with the USSR, a product of Cold War politics when India and the USSR had a strong strategic relationship. The PSU deputed him to Russia for two years under the technology transfer programme. It worried Biva as the Sino-Indian War was just ended and Chandan was in class ten (10). Cold fear spiralled through her because of remarks made by relatives and neighbours. Khagendra kept his family in the Dumdum in his father-in-law's house and went to Moscow. Biva watched Dum Dum again and it was a real blast from the past. Chandan got admitted to a local school with the help of his maternal grandfather. At the time of Chandan's higher secondary Examination in 1965, Khagendra returned from Russia and shifted his family from Dum Dum to Durgapur. The family was housed in the Company's allotted quarters.

Gandhi's doctrines and ideology influenced Khagendra during his youth when he closely watched Gandhi at their ancestral home. As he grew older, he became disillusioned with Congress and its politics, and his Congress bubble burst. We all have an ideological bubble, but all bubbles have a way of bursting or being deflated at the end.

In the USSR, Khagendra was perplexed to see; the Russians lived under a totalitarian regime. People were afraid to speak or discuss anything about state or politics, fearing political repression and mass surveillance. He was bitterly disappointed about left-wing politics, as the Communist Party of the Soviet Union was the mother of the Indian Communist Party. M. N. Roy and others formed CPI in 1920 in Russia.

Nikita Khrushchev was the Soviet leader during Khagendra's stay in Russia. He denounced Stalin's purges or great terror when millions of people were executed or sent to Siberia. But he was removed from power in 1964 and replaced by Leonid Brezhnev. Cold War existed between the western bloc and the Soviet bloc. In society, we were fed communist/right-wing propaganda. The whole nation was force-fed government propaganda about how well the country/state was doing.

But in India, it was the post-colonial period. The developed countries used capital, globalization and conditional aid to influence a developing country instead of the earlier colonial method of direct control. Capitalist powers (both national and multinational) controlled the economy of Third World countries. Our country was depended on eastern and western blocks for capital inflows (FDI and FPI), military requirements, industries, and technological up-gradations, even for food.

India relied on food supplies from the USA under PL480 against rupees' payments. Jawaharlal Nehru was the first Prime Minister of India since independence until he died in 1964, and political dynasties or political families emerged in Indian politics thereafter. In 2014 Lok Sabha, 22 percent of MPs have a dynastic background, and in Congress, 48 percent of its current MPs of India are dynast. Politics is now a "closed shop" for educated professionals and tax-paying middle class. There is a perception among the tax-paying class that politics is dirty and full of corruption.

From 1966 and onwards, Khagendra and his family used to consume Chapattis made from flour, or Atta, as a principal food. The sixties were a decade of prosperity and abundance in the Western world and the USA. It was the best of times in the developed world, but it was the worst of times for us. In India, people were busy trying to stay alive. Very few could afford some comfort or luxuries. We remained dependent on external aid and had *to cope with a lack of infrastructure, lack of equipment, lack of food, lack of medicines, and a lack of understanding of hygiene by the population.* Dozens of people queued for all morning in front of the ration shop to buy food-grains and sugar. Chandan, like other boys, stood in a queue for a long hour, waiting patiently to purchase weekly ration from the Public distribution system. But it was not enough to meet the consumption needs of the families.

Second Generation - Indian Born Children of Foreign-Born Parents

In 1965, Chandan passed the Higher Secondary Examination with 1st Division marks at 15 plus age. He enrolled in the Burdwan Raj College for the B. Sc Physics Honours course and stayed in the college hostel. It was the first time; he was outside his family and its protected environment. He was shy and conservative in outlook. In a quick time, he became easy with his new way of life. The hosteler sat for hours talking about everything under the sun, but the women, cinemas, football, and politics were hotly debated topics. But the students had trouble retaining their optimism. Gone was the pervasive optimism of early 1960. The students got angry observing income disparity, wealth inequality, abject poverty, money in politics, and corporate influence in the government. They were disenchanted with the state of existing political systems. It was time for a new narrative. It was a time of Naxalbari Uprising.

Zakir was Chandan's roommate in the hostel. He belonged to a peasant family of Paraj in Galsi 1 block and a devout Muslim. Religion became a day in and day out obsession for him.

Chandan told him one day, "Why are you so religious? I am born as a Hindu but not a practising Hindu." Zakir informed Chandan that they were Salafi Muslims. Chandan asked what that was. Zakir informed Sunnis and Shias were two main Muslim communities in India. There were distinct branches within Sunni Islams as Deobandi, Barelvi, Salafis, Wahhabis, and Wahhabi Salafis.

Chandan said, yes in our religion, there were also distinct branches of devotees, my maternal Grand Father was Vaishnava (follower of Krishna), my father was Shakta (worshipper of the Divine Mother), but my mother believed in all Gods and Goddess, I was an agnostic and a few of my relatives were an atheist. In Hindu religion, there was no single prophet, there was no single God, it did not follow anyone acts of religious rites; it did not believe anyone's philosophic concept, if anybody did not believe in the existence of God or any rules or ritual, and they were still Hindu.

Zakir told Chandan, religion had always been uppermost in the mind of Muslims and for Salafi Muslim., they dominated it in their everyday life. Chandan recited a couplet of Sufi, Fariduddin Attar.

"Polytheists, monotheists, atheists, fire and idol worshippers, all are in my folders/the only condition is to have a heart of gold."

In 1967, Share Croppers and small farmers upraised against the local landlord in the Naxalbari Block in the Siliguri subdivision where 50 to 60 percentages of tillers were Sharecroppers. They had started a movement from 1965 to 66, and it reached its peak when an armed agent of the landlord beat a tiller in 1967. The sharecroppers and marginal farmers under the leadership of Naxal leaders retaliated by annihilating the landed classes and captured the land and crops of landlords. The revolutionary idea of armed peasant revolt to change the system spread like fire throughout Bengal, and in the Indian political scene, a new political ideology came in the Indian political map.

Chandan was an ardent reader of post-Rabindranath literature and the enthusiastic watcher of group-theatre and new wave cinema. He became involved with the publication of Little Magazine. It was the then-latest craze. He also contributed articles for the college wall magazine. Then, a Hungry generation movement took the cultural movement by a storm that disturbed readers' pre-conceived colonial canons. All these influenced Chandan, and he drifted further away from his studies. He sustained a hairline fracture of the wrist in an inter-college football match and his hand was in plaster for about six weeks.

Love comes as a much-needed refresher in Chandan's life; it brought an *unfamiliar* feeling to him. It resembled a fever; only the person falling in love could feel it. He had unexplainable, powerful feelings for someone. He felt a strong desire for a Hindu Panjabi youthful woman who was their next-door neighbour in their Durgapur quarters. Chandan homecoming from the hostel became frequent. He liked her, wanted to say it to her, but he could not say a word. It scared him to propose fearing rejection.

The lady was pretty and had a husky voice. Chandan impressed with her gentle femininity. She did not continue her study after 10 classes and was busy with household chores with her mother. Chandan found her very attractive. Biva and the lady's mother became a friend, and they exchanged their respective, culinary. Biva gave them Bengali cuisine and in return got Punjabi dishes. They remained friends through various challenges.

The lady's mother had a baby girl at 45 years. After giving birth, being older, she felt embarrassed. The baby was very healthy and looked like a fat Barbie doll. Chandan liked the child, and whenever he got a chance, he took the baby to his room. The youthful woman came to the Chandan room to collect her sister. She also came to Biva's house with her mother for chattering in leisure time. The youthful woman and Chandan met frequently, but they did not talk to each other. When they met, they did not also gaze at each other but looked outward in the same direction. The lady's family left Durgapur unexpectedly for her father's sudden transfer of service to Tamil Nadu.

Chandan arrived home from the hostel with a resolution that he would talk with the woman. But he saw the woman's house remained locked; he assumed they had gone somewhere for a brief tour or to their hometown in Punjab. After a few days, he came back home with an expectation that the woman's family might have returned home by now. To his great surprise, he saw a new family lived in the flat.

He asked his mother about them. Biva said the company transferred the lady's father in a site office in South India, where the Company got a turnkey project. The next day, Chandan returned to his hostel, and he was crestfallen. It was hard for Chandan to forget the woman. He told his friends; "I will discover the lady and she will be my girl". Chandan could not trace the lady and remained unmarried for the rest of his life.

At graduation, he had a compartment in pass subject chemistry which he cleared next year. He did not get a chance for a post-graduate course at any university. The employment market was bad during the late sixties. There was hardly any job in the job market for ordinary science graduates. He applied for several jobs, got interview calls for a few, but did not get any job offer. It was then a widely held view that job seekers needed an insider help to get a job.

One year after graduation, he got a temporary teaching job in a higher secondary school as a physics teacher at leave vacancy posts. After one year, he became unemployed again. On parental pressure, he enrolled for AMIE courses, but became depressed like the other unemployed, considering their bleak prospects. The country's economy was not encouraging, unemployment was high and the country was mired in chaos and widespread corruption.

It was the Bengal of the seventies. Students and youths were in rebellion against the current political system. Thousands of students from the city's leading educational institutes joined with the Naxal movement. Annihilation of police constables, small moneylenders, and tiny landholders as class enemies of people took place in villages, mofussil towns, and Calcutta. Police tortured Naxalite followers and killed them in cold blood. Anybody suspected by police as Naxal was arrested and tortured in the name of investigation. Tension and fear were everywhere. Nobody dared to move beyond their safety zone. Bengal became a battleground among students, youths, and police administration. The government crushed the rebellion with a brute force. Political parties irrespective of right or left were against the Naxal movement, but the filmmakers made intellectual films, poets, and novelists had written mind-boggling poetries and novels, based on the Naxal uprising from a distant safe place.

The Revolution Will Not Be Televised.

"You will not be able to stay home, brother
You will not be able to plug-in, turn on, and cop-out
You will not be able to lose yourself on skag.
And skip out for beer during commercials
Because the revolution will not be televised.

The revolution will not be televised
The revolution will not be brought to you by Xerox.
In 4 parts, without commercial interruptions."

– by Gil Scott-Heron

And then, after months of discussion, Chandan formed an Engineers' Industrial Co-operative Society in Durgapur with a few diploma engineers hoping to build business on working on government contractor jobs. But, after the Cooperative's formation, they observed, winning a Government work was painstaking, long, competitive and it needed pre tender preparation works, time and money. Initially, they did not get any works as government agencies viewed past performance as one of the key criteria to select a contractor. So, the society tried to get smaller project at first as it would create job credentials for them. As, there was no work and no money, all members of the society left except the secretary, president, treasurer, and two executive members. Chandan worked as the Society's secretary.

After a year, the Co-operative Society got its first civil work for construction of a boundary wall of a park. They could not execute the work profitably for lack of experience and organizational synergies. Some days later, they realized, the easiest way to win government works was to grease the palms of the correct men in the right place.

Knowing the secret to win the Government's contract works, the Co-operative used to get government works. They applied for office space and industrial plot to local Govt of Durgapur. The society got an office spaces at the Durgapur City Centre and 2-acre vacant lands to set up a small scale industry at Durgapur on a 60-year lease basis. They expanded their business within a brief period and took on rent two Guest Houses, one in Salt Lake, Calcutta, and others in Delhi.

Society took loans from Burdwan Central Co-Operative Bank, Durgapur, against government work orders for their working capital needs and establishment costs. SBI and UCO Bank also sanctioned loans to society against their work orders. The society was growing thick and fast and increased the number of staff on its payroll.

They got civil construction works of the Tehri Dam project in Uttarakhand. The society bagged the civil works of the Uranium Corporation of India's Township at Jadugora. They won the contracts of many roads and highway construction projects of major Govt bodies like NHAI, PWD, CPWD, DDA, and various Municipal Corporations. The society was running effortlessly for 10 to 12 years.

The Society suffered an enormous loss in the Korba Super Thermal Power Project of NTPC in Chhattisgarh because of a few employees, Society trusted embezzled company's fund. Thereafter, the society's business was in steep decline. As they could not complete the project at a scheduled time, as a result, the society was blacklisted from the NTPC's works. The Banks issued a notice to the Society to payback of their loan. The situation created an one-two punch to Society with a cash crunch and recall of advance by the bank. It forced them to close their two Guest Houses. They were in debt to their suppliers as well. But the society did not lay off any staff except those who were involved in the embezzlement of society's funds. Society did some low-budget works to overcome financial difficulties. They reconstructed the Minerva cinema hall to Chaplin hall at Esplanade in Kolkata in 1980 and did some construction works in Garden Reach Shipbuilders and Engineering Ltd. Navigating business at trouble time was a tricky thing. Society was down, but not out of the business.

Khagendra retired from service on reaching the age of 58 years as an office Superintendent and became free from the bureaucratic bungling of the Government job. He refused re-employment offers from different private firms. Since retiring from the company, he had involved in voluntary charity works. Khagendra shifted his family from the company's quarters to a rented house near the old Township. Sanchayita, a Ponzi scheme, was then a popular Chit fund company, and an agent of the Chit Fund was chasing Khagendra for investment in their chit fund. Khagendra could not resist the lure of 48% interest. He invested some amount of his retirement benefits of them, but the chit fund company was crushed within a few months after his investment.

Biva's father lived with his son-in-law in Durgapur at his advanced age; he was a devoted Chaitanya Vaishnavas and spent his time studying the Vaishnava Padavali and the Hindu Scripture books. He had an enormous collection of Hindu texts, mainly literature on Vaishnavism. He chanted a set of hymns from the scriptures. He found peace through meditation and enjoyed singing hymns to Esraj, sometimes; he sang without accompanying instruments. At the fag end of his life, he became blind and withdrawn from his spiritual activities, which were his mainstay for the last 60 years. He now invested time in deep involvement for life. Now, he had no goal, no want, no longing, no past, no future, no art, no method, just waiting in silence without resistance for the ultimate day. It was 'letting go' practice. He died in sleep at the Brahma- muhurta (last quarter of the night) in 1980.

Khagendra left Durgapur and shifted his family to Dum Dum a few years after his father-in-law's death. Biva's father rented out the Dum Dum house to a refugee family on meagre rent who fled from Noakhali in 1965, on condition that the refugee family vacated the house when he returned Dum Dum after his son-in-law's retirement. After Khagendra's retirement, Biva's father requested the tenant to vacate the house, but they did not. Khagendra then filed an eviction suit, but the court rejected their plaint after 8 years of trial according to an archaic tenancy act. The refugee family asked for a lump sum of money for vacating the house. Khagendra took possession of the house after fulfilling their demands. The house at Dum Dum was an old-fashioned; the kitchen and toilet were far off from the bedrooms. They repaired and reallocated the kitchen and bathroom as best as possible.

Chandan stayed in Durgapur at his office at the Durgapur City Centre. He built a big farmhouse on the industrial plot. He used to come to Dumdum after a long gap. As and when he came to Dum Dum, he came late at night. In his presence, it changed the family atmosphere; family members switched all lights of the building on, and Biva prepared food for Chandan. He brought food packets, milk, coffee, snacks, Cadbury chocolate bars, toiletries, facial creams for his niece and sister-in-law. All items were in large and multiple in numbers. Chandan's homecoming was a joyous occasion. He did not give regular financial contributions to his family, but he bore the educational expenses of many poor medicals and engineering students. He also helped poor people for their medical treatment and assisted the helpless fathers for their daughter's marriage.

He had always had a soft spot on his young nephew and niece and used to give them costly gifts. He had an unconventional lifestyle and dared to live on his terms. Once upon a time, he was a job seeker, but now he was a job creator and employer of so many staff members. Once before the Durga Puja, he purchased 100 Katha stitch silk sarees and 100 Katha stitch Tussar long Kurta to give it as a Puja gift to his staff, their families and his family, including their maidservants. One of his passions was sharing food with others. He was a vegetarian and cooked his foods himself, though he started a restaurant below his residence. 20 boys were working in the restaurant; Chandan distributed Cadbury Chocolate to these boys in the evening. Occasionally, he went to Asansol Fruit Market by car and came back with carload Mangoes and distributed the fruits to neighbours and the boys working in the restaurant. He wore very modest clothes. Government officials thought Chandan was a low-level employee of the farm at their first meeting.

In the 90s, Biva became very sick. Then, Khagendra wanted to engage a full-time female help for housework and requested Chandan to make the arrangements. Chandan told his staff to hire a female help for his home who did not have any family obligations. One of his employees requested his village Gram Panchayats to provide an aged, widowed woman as a housemaid at their boss's home. Panchayat arranged a woman from their village for that job. The elderly lady went to the Chandan temporary office with that man. When she saw Chandan; she felt dejected to see her new master as the man looked like a poor man as any poor man in her village. The elderly lady remained with the family for 20 years until Biva's death.

The doctor diagnosed Khagendra with Lymphoma cancer during his sunset period of life, and there were few things more alarming than fighting cancer. Cancer is an extreme situation for a cancer patient's loved one. Because of improvements in cancer treatment, the survival rate has increased. These remarkable advances also mean that treatments come at an exorbitant price.

Before he got cancer, he suffered from acute constipation. Family members admitted him three times in Nursing Homes for different ailments. He died on 28th August 2001 at the nursing home after a year-long fight with cancer. The physical form of Khagendra became void.

"Gate gate pāragate pārasamgate Bodhi svāhā."

– Prajna Paramita, Heart Sutra

(Gone, /Gone, /Gone over. /Gone fully over. /Awakened! /So be it!

The Heart Sutra states, "Form is empty, emptiness is form." It is a Buddhist Mahayana teaching which states; ultimately all phenomena are sunya or empty or void.

Everything, whatever we see, one day it will be over, nothing is permanent, every phase of our life makes us busy, but it's transitional, everything will end one day, and all things whatever it may be, at the end are empty and void.

All that we see is but a dream within a dream.

– Edgar Allan Poe

Chandan, after his father's death, won a few big Government works such as the residential complex of 24 high-rise buildings for Calcutta Metropolitan Development Authority (CMDA) in Patuli, a hospital in Bangaon, and a few enormous projects in North Bengal. He started a new Restaurant, Diner Inn, in Durgapur City Centre, just below his office cum residence, and it did a roaring business within a brief period.

The Society was hoping for a big breakthrough in the year 2006 when the farm got the contract of the two road-rail bridges of Eastern Railway in Bihar having an enormous project cost.

Chandan was making necessary arrangements for the recent Railway projects at his Durgapur Office. On the morning of 3rd June 2006, he felt a sharp pain in the chest. He presumed the pain was for gas and took the gas relief medicine, but the pain did not subside. Friends and employees forced him to visit a local doctor.

The doctor did an ECG test to check his heart condition and advised him to admit to the hospital. Chandan at once rushed to the Durgapur Steel Plant Hospital (DSP), which was then the only hospital in Durgapur.

The hospital admitted him and kept him to the hospital's ICU on Saturday evening. At the weekend, no senior doctors were on duty except an RMO who was a junior doctor. The backup medical services were not also available. We observed the thousand of the patients died every year after being admitted to the hospital on the weekend.

On the 4th June, Sunday morning, employees of the farm informed Chandan's family at Dumdum of his illness.

At their inquiry about his health condition, they informed them that he was in DSP Hospital and now his condition was stable. When his younger brother reached Durgapur from Dum Dum in the afternoon, the ICU nurse advised him to come at 5.00 p.m. during visiting hour. At 5 p.m., when he was on the staircase, RMO called the relative of Chandan and advised him to give water in Chandan's mouth, as he was about to die. His brother gave water to Chandan's lips. His eyes fluttered open for a moment, and he breathed his last that afternoon. At Chandan's bedside, Chandan's brother learned what death looked like. His hands and feet became cold. The eyes were turned backwards. Chandan now got closer to God, "Nearer, my God, to Thee, Nearer to Thee." He was just 56 years old. It reminds us, we only have limited time. Chandan's younger brother was worried how he delivered the news of his older brother's death to his mother and others in Dumdum over the phone. He finally plucked up the courage and conveyed the sad news to Dumdum that Chandan was no more.

Friends and employees of his farm brought him from the hospital to a restaurant. Now, Chandan lay on his restaurant table, his body wrapped in a white linen sheet. *The* body *was in an* early stage *of decomposition.* Restaurant's working boys and staff were inconsolable after the death of Chandan.

The family members came to Durgapur for his last rites from Dumdum. On the 5th June morning, cremation took place at the local crematorium in Durgapur in the presence of his staff, friends, neighbours and a handicapped woman whom Chandan gave employment and helped her to get married. She was sobbing uncontrollably near the Chandan's funeral pyre. She worked as a manager of the restaurant.

After the cremation of the body, family members went to his office cum residence in the City Centre. It surprised them to see, Chandan had no belongings except a few old shirts and pants. He had no Bank account in his name, though he was in business for the last 35 years and spent money during that period like a drunken sailor. Even more surprising that he had no Almirah or trunk or suitcase in his room, only a cot was there. There was a tea shop near his house cum office in the city centre, and anybody could have tea from that shop in the name of Chandan. At the month's end, Chandan used to foot the bill, which sometimes crossed ten thousand rupees. All the employees cried as if they lost everything. Society, after Chandan's death, could not do the Railways contract and the Co-operative became defunct. The eatery is functioning, and surviving partners depend on the income from the Restaurant for their livelihood. But they are being hounded by Bank staff and the Employees' Provident Fund Authority for repayment of their overdue Bank's loans and arrears PFs of their employees.

Biva could not accept Chandan's death. She plunged into grief and despair. She got angry at God. She blamed God for it because if God truly cared, He wouldn't let her suffer. She believed that Chandan could not die. It was what she wanted to believe. She observed Chandan outside the house, but he did not come inside the home. She stood in the balcony every morning and waited for a man who used the road in front of their house as a pass-through. According to Biva, the man was Chandan in disguise. It became an obsession with her. She withdrew from the family affair and sat silently on the couch.

The lady, whom Chandan brought into the house, said Chandan's ghost often appeared in the house. Her lower lip trembled and she cried. But other family members could see nothing strange.

Biva became a patient of faecal incontinence, and the village woman did everything to clean her from time to time. Biva was plagued by ill health throughout her life because of chronic bacillary dysentery. Advanced age aggravated the disease. She suffered a stroke and other ailments earlier and admitted to the company's hospital in Durgapur and Nursing homes in Calcutta several times. In the past, she survived so many crises, but she lost her battle in 2010.

She died in her sleep on April 10, 2010. At last, Biva saw Chandan at her bedside, Biva's last words- Chandan! Chandan guided his mother to her afterlife journey.

Epilogue

The above narrative was a record of past events that happened or ended a long time ago and was not important now. The above note was genuine and was a description of a particular place and a few people. These persons are not important now, although they were in the past. It was also a record of terrible experiences, East Bengal Hindus experienced over a lengthy period with no fault of them. The past events are considered together, events of a particular period to understand the current shape of the country and why things came about the way they did.

The characters, narrated, had played their roles and left our world. Each character has two dates, one for birth and another for death, but all that is important is events that happened between these two dates and it shapes the past and present course of our history. The present joy, sorrow and suffering, it is often said, are the product of the past.

The royal family referred to 1946 and onwards as years of horrors. 1947 may go down in East Bengal refugees' life as their annus horribilis. The situation compelled them to come and they came to Calcutta and experienced tough times for the decision of a few. They struggled against adversity and did not hang their head down. We are still alive, but all my characters with which my story engaged for so long were dead, God only knows who was right and who was wrong for all the incidents happened since 1203 A. D. People come, people go and things are right or wrong, but life goes on.

Our insignificance and bubble-like temporary life were best described by Thomas Gray.

I take this great quote from the ninth stanza of Thomas Gray's poem' Elegy' *Written in a Country Churchyard.*

"The boast of heraldry, the pomp of power, and all that beauty, all that wealth ever gave, Awaits alike th' inevitable hour,

The paths of glory lead, but to the grave."

References

1. *Google Search.*

2. *Noakhalir itihash by Pyarimohan Sen 1ˢᵗ Published in 1876*

3. *Noakhali O Swandwiper itihash compiled and edited by Komal Choudhury; Published by Dey'sPublishing.*

4. *Family Tree by Birendra Narayan Roy Prepared in 1958*

5. *Family Information:-*

   a) Dilip Narayan Roy (Barda)

   b) Prabir Narayan Roy

6. *My Days with Gandhi by Nirmal Kumar Bose*

7. *Full Text of Noakhali–Internet Archive*

8. *Banglapedia*

9. *Time of India English daily newspaper.*